W9-AQD-824

CREATIVE HOMEOWNER®

ULTIMATE GUIDE TO

Kids' Play Structures and Tree Houses

10 EASY-TO-BUILD, FUN PROJECTS

Jeff Beneke

CREATIVE HOMEOWⁿ   iver, New Jersey

ULTIMATE GUIDE TO KIDS' PLAY STRUCTURES AND TREE HOUSES

AUTHORS	Jeff Beneke, Original Edition; Steve Willson, New Material
MANAGING EDITOR	Fran Donegan
GRAPHIC DESIGNER	Kathryn Wityk
PHOTO COORDINATOR	Robyn Poplasky
JUNIOR EDITOR	Jennifer Calvert
EDITORIAL ASSISTANTS	Nora Grace, Sara Markowitz
DIGITAL IMAGING SPECIALIST	Frank Dyer
PRODUCTION INTERN	Michelle Kalinski
INDEXER	Schroeder Indexing Services
COVER DESIGN	Kathryn Wityk
ILLUSTRATIONS	Paul M. Schumm; Craig Franklin; Vincent Alessi; Tom Klenck, new material
COVER PHOTOGRAPHY	All by CH, except: (front top left) iStockphoto.com/Mary Marin

CREATIVE HOMEOWNER

VICE PRESIDENT AND PUBLISHER	Timothy O. Bakke
PRODUCTION DIRECTOR	Kimberly H. Vivas
ART DIRECTOR	David Geer
MANAGING EDITOR	Fran J. Donegan

Current Printing (last digit)
10 9 8 7 6 5 4 3 2 1

Ultimate Guide to Kids' Play Structures and Tree Houses, Second Edition
Library of Congress Control Number: 2008921439
ISBN-10: 1-58011-422-9
ISBN-13: 978-1-58011-422-6

Manufactured in the United States of America

CREATIVE HOMEOWNER®
A Division of Federal Marketing Corp.
24 Park Way
Upper Saddle River, NJ 07458
www.creativehomeowner.com

Planet Friendly Publishing
✔ Made in the United States
✔ Printed on Recycled Paper
Learn more at www.greenedition.org

GREEN EDITION

At Creative Homeowner we're committed to producing books in an earth-friendly manner and to helping our customers make greener choices.

Manufacturing books in the United States ensures compliance with strict environmental laws and eliminates the need for international freight shipping, a major contributor to global air pollution.

And printing on recycled paper helps minimize our consumption of trees, water, and fossil fuels. *Ultimate Guide to Kids' Play Structures and Tree Houses* was printed on paper made with 10% post-consumer waste. According to Environmental Defense's Paper Calculator, by using this innovative paper instead of conventional papers, we achieved the following environmental benefits:

Trees Saved: 16

Water Saved: 5,956 gallons

Solid Waste Eliminated: 985 pounds

Air Emissions Eliminated: 1,817 pounds

For more information on our environmental practices, please visit us online at www.creativehomeowner.com/green

safety

Although the methods in this book have been reviewed for safety, it is not possible to overstate the importance of using the safest methods you can. What follows are reminders—some do's and don'ts of work safety—to use along with your common sense.

▌ Always use caution, care, and good judgment when following the procedures described in this book.

▌ Always be sure that the electrical setup is safe, that no circuit is overloaded, and that all power tools and outlets are properly grounded. Do not use power tools in wet locations.

▌ Always read container labels on paints, solvents, and other products; provide ventilation; and observe all other warnings.

▌ Always read the manufacturer's instructions for using a tool, especially the warnings.

▌ Use hold-downs and push sticks whenever possible when working on a table saw. Avoid working short pieces if you can.

▌ Always remove the key from any drill chuck (portable or press) before starting the drill.

▌ Always pay deliberate attention to how a tool works so that you can avoid being injured.

▌ Always know the limitations of your tools. Do not try to force them to do what they were not designed to do.

▌ Always make sure that any adjustment is locked before proceeding. For example, always check the rip fence on a table saw or the bevel adjustment on a portable saw before starting to work.

▌ Always clamp small pieces to a bench or other work surface when using a power tool.

▌ Always wear the appropriate rubber gloves or work gloves when handling chemicals, moving or stacking lumber, working with concrete, or doing heavy construction.

▌ Always wear a disposable face mask when you create dust by sawing or sanding. Use a special filtering respirator when working with toxic substances and solvents.

▌ Always wear eye protection, especially when using power tools or striking metal on metal or concrete; a chip can fly off, for example, when chiseling concrete.

▌ Never work while wearing loose clothing, open cuffs, or jewelry; tie back long hair.

▌ Always be aware that there is seldom enough

time for your body's reflexes to save you from injury from a power tool in a dangerous situation; everything happens too fast. Be alert!

▌ Always keep your hands away from the business ends of blades, cutters, and bits.

▌ Always hold a circular saw firmly, usually with both hands.

▌ Always use a drill with an auxiliary handle to control the torque when using large-size bits.

▌ Always check your local building codes when planning new construction. The codes are intended to protect public safety and should be observed to the letter.

▌ Never work with power tools when you are tired, or when under the influence of alcohol or drugs.

▌ Never cut tiny pieces of wood or pipe using a power saw. When you need a small piece, saw it from a securely clamped longer piece.

▌ Never change a saw blade or a drill or router bit unless the power cord is unplugged. Do not depend on the switch being off. You might accidentally hit it.

▌ Never work in insufficient lighting.

▌ Never work with dull tools. Have them sharpened, or learn how to sharpen them yourself.

▌ Never use a power tool on a workpiece—large or small—that is not firmly supported.

▌ Never saw a workpiece that spans a large distance between horses without close support on each side of the cut; the piece can bend, closing on and jamming the blade, causing saw kickback.

▌ When sawing, never support a workpiece from underneath with your leg or any other part of your body.

▌ Never carry sharp or pointed tools, such as utility knives, awls, or chisels, in your pocket. If you want to carry any of these tools, use a special-purpose tool belt that has leather pockets and holders.

contents

INTRODUCTION
playing & learning

Few sights are more pleasant than children at play—running, jumping, climbing, and swinging as though life had no other purpose. Although play is usually carefree, it is much more than a mere release of energy.

Like the classroom and library, the play yard can be a center for learning and other vital development. In fact, play is an important component of a lifelong process of learning.

EVERYONE BENEFITS

Play, in its many forms, greatly contributes to a child's physical, cognitive, and social development.

The most obvious benefit of a play yard is physical exercise. Here a child can improve coordination, motor skills, strength, agility, balance, and endurance.

The play yard also stimulates a child's imagination and requires problem solving. And during group play, children learn verbal and other socialization skills, such as cooperating, sharing, and group decision making. These experiences help a child outgrow the self-centeredness of infancy and become more considerate.

Besides benefiting children, a play structure rewards its builder. Your "labor of love" can provide immense personal satisfaction. And because play structures will be used and appreciated for years, they will continue to reward you.

All projects in this book were designed for durability, safety, and enjoyment. A durable structure withstands the elements, as well as the punishment of active children. A safe structure minimizes potential for injuries and includes impact-reducing materials, such as wood chips or pea gravel, to cushion falls and landings. As for enjoyment, these projects have proven "kid appeal."

The Kids' Playland, with its Central Tower, Swing Beam, and Monkey Bar, allows you to customize the layout to available space and to the ages and interests of your kids. It also gives you options for building in stages—one module at a time.

Other projects include the Playhouse, the Picnic Table, the Teeter-Totter, and a relatively simple sandbox. If you want to begin gradually, perhaps to build confidence in your abilities, begin with one of the simpler projects. You can even include your children in the planning of the structure for a fun family project.

Beginning with Chapter 6, each chapter opens with an illustration of the completed project and an illustration with an information box that indicates difficulty level and tools required. For some of the projects, the difficulty

GUIDE TO SKILL LEVEL

 Easy. Even for beginners.

 Challenging. Can be done by beginners who have the patience and willingness to learn.

 Difficult. Can be handled by most experienced do-it-yourselfers who have mastered basic construction skills. Consider consulting a specialist.

level is represented by one, two, or three hammers, as shown in box, left.

The final three projects, a Victorian-style playhouse and two tree houses, are more advanced and should be considered three-hammer projects. While challenging, the detailed illustrations and written instructions will help you tackle these projects. The playhouse is extremely intricate, so careful measuring is a must. When working on the tree houses, remember that you may be doing much of the work off of the ground, so safety considerations should be your first priority.

You will often have the option of using either hand or power tools. For example, you may prefer to use hand drills, rather than an electric drill, for easier projects. So the information box may simply indicate "drilling tools," rather than indicate a preference. Illustrations throughout each project chapter and in Chapter 4, on techniques, show virtually all tool options.

PART ONE

This part of the book will help you plan and design your play yard, select the right materials, and offer building techniques to help you complete the projects in this book. The projects include the "Kids' Playland," which is a traditional backyard play structure that consists of a Central Tower with a slide, a Swing Beam, and a Monkey Bar. There are also more advanced projects that include a playhouse and two tree houses that you can build.

We heartily recommend that everyone in the family be involved in planning and design, but we don't recommend that only the adults participate in the construction itself.

MATERIALS & METHODS

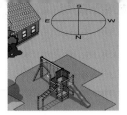

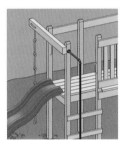

1 planning and design

The end result may be play, but the process of planning and designing a play structure should not be taken lightly. A play structure will make significant, possibly long term, changes in the appearance and function of your yard. It will also require a significant investment of money and time, so you want a finished project that looks good, functions properly, and lasts. The best way to achieve these objectives is to plan carefully.

Consider the kind of structure you want and can afford, as well as the best location in your yard. Will you be doing the work yourself? How will the final structure affect your view and that of your neighbors? Even a modest play structure can affect a property's attractiveness and function.

PLANNING AHEAD

Kids have a seemingly inexhaustible need for play. Even toddlers, with notoriously short attention spans, can remain content for long periods on a playground that offers a variety of appropriate diversions and challenges. Of course, as the children age and require less and less direct supervision, they develop preferences for new types of playground activities. But their need for play doesn't diminish.

Therefore, one of the design challenges is to find ways to incorporate a range of activities that can interest the youngest and oldest kids alike. Pre-schoolers have different physical and cognitive abilities from school kids. To ensure long-term use, the structures must "mature" in their offerings along with your children.

To achieve this objective, there are two options: you could build a big, multifunctional Kids' Play Structure now, containing all of the components you anticipate needing in years to come. Or you could go modular by building only what your kids would like now, with the intention of adapting and adding components later.

This book is organized to allow for either of the above two options. For example, you could build an elevated Central Tower with a slide now. Later, you could add the Swing Frame. As your kids become old enough, you might want to tack on the Monkey Bar or build it and the Swing Frame to stand alone. Think of the advanced playhouse and two tree houses as separate projects from the play structure.

KIDS' PLAYLAND AND OTHER PROJECTS

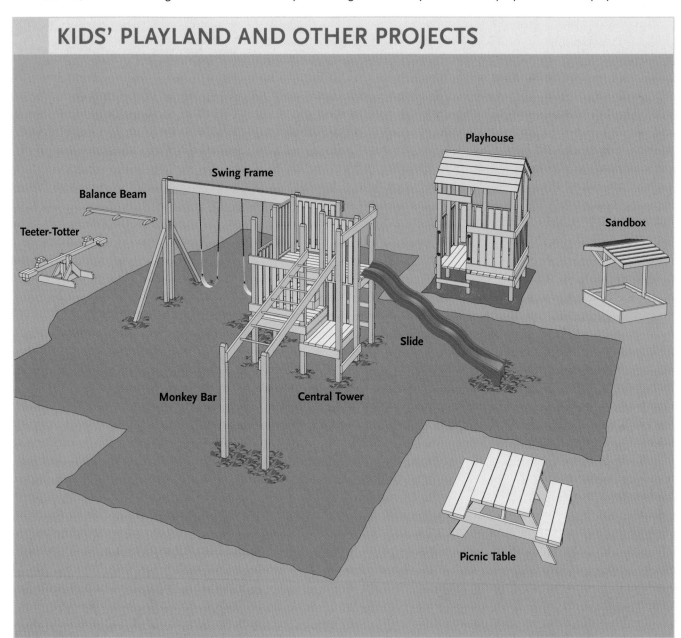

Playhouse

Swing Frame

Balance Beam

Teeter-Totter

Sandbox

Slide

Monkey Bar

Central Tower

Picnic Table

If you have doubts about what to build first, take your kids to a busy public playground and just watch. Also, study kids of various ages. See what they enjoy most, and what they are capable of or have difficulty with. One thing you will notice is that kids don't generally play with one component or in one spot for long periods. Rather, they move from one component to another. There is an important lesson in this; if given only one activity, kids will get bored. It's important to give them lots of choices.

CHOOSING THE SITE

For many families, there aren't many site options for a play structure. Your biggest challenge may be fitting your planned project into a small area. The site should be relatively level and, ideally, shouldn't interfere much with the other uses for your yard, such as picnics, games, pet runs, and relaxation. Although the backyard is usually the best location for most structures, don't automatically rule out the front yard or a side yard location that is visible from the street, if local codes allow it.

Creating Safe Spacing. Even if your siting choices are limited, it is still important to allow plenty of space for each structure, as well as "elbow room" for safe play, without overlooking the other functions of the yard. If your space is tight, you would probably be wiser to build just the Central Tower with enough free space around it than to attempt to squeeze more modules in.

Keep play structures well away from roads, sidewalks, and any other natural pathways that are likely to have people on them. This is especially important with regard to the Swing Frame: don't let the path of swing intersect a pedestrian pathway. On newer public playgrounds, you will probably notice that the swings are isolated from the other parts of the playground. This improves playground safety by keeping the swingers away from other activities. Even if you've got little room in your yard, be sure to consider safety zoning. Likewise, position the exit chute of a slide to minimize the chance of sliding into traffic.

If you are building for preschoolers, remember that they need to be supervised or at least watched within calling distance. You may also want to choose a spot that allows a supervisor to sit comfortably, out of the sun.

Considering Sun and Wind. Environmental and physical factors that affect the amount and type of light, the velocity and direction of wind, and the effect of percipitation may determine your siting.

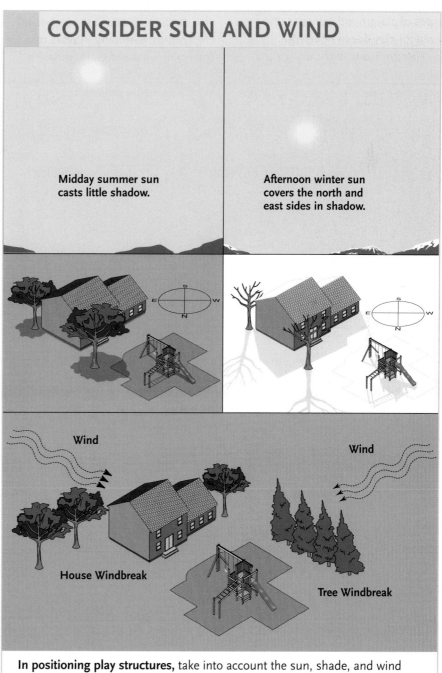

CONSIDER SUN AND WIND

Midday summer sun casts little shadow.

Afternoon winter sun covers the north and east sides in shadow.

Wind

Wind

House Windbreak

Tree Windbreak

In positioning play structures, take into account the sun, shade, and wind through the seasons.

When you have a rough idea of the style of play structure you like, you need to decide which way it will face. For this, consider the effects of sun and shade.

A play structure in an unshaded location may become quite a hot spot in summer. For example, if you plan to install a metal slide, you may want to situate it on a northerly side to minimize its heating in the sun. At the same time, you probably won't want the structure entirely in the shade. So try to find a site that provides a good balance of sun and shade. Remember, the location and angle of the sun will change through the seasons. Although the low-angle winter sun may cast longer shadows in your yard, the high-angle summer sun may strike more of the play structure.

If your yard is subject to strong winds, consider possibilities for wind protection. For example, try to find a site that is downwind of a line of trees, or even your house. If wind is a problem, create some relatively wind-free sanctuaries within the structure.

Footprint with Safety Zones. The full space requirement for the kid's playland includes the footprint of the components themselves, plus the safety zones extending from each. The illustrations below and on the next page show possible configurations. Ideally, all of the zones should be filled with impact-reducing material, such as wood mulch or pea gravel, to depths recommended in the table "Impact-Reducing Materials" on page 35. The illustration below shows that the playland, with safety zones, needs a large footprint. Following this recommendation, you ensure that impact-reducing material would soften the landing of a child falling or jumping from any part of the play structure, including extended swing arcs.

FOOTPRINT WITH SAFETY ZONES

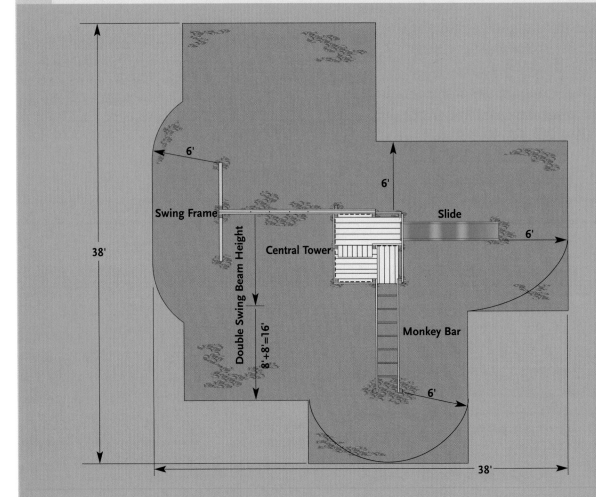

For safety, extend an impact-reducing material, such as wood chips or pea gravel, at least 6 feet out from all parts of the structure and at least double the farthest reach of the arc of the swings.

PREPARING A SITE PLAN

Once you have a rough idea of the type structure you want, the best way to visualize how much yard it will occupy is to make a scaled drawing, called a site plan. For this you can use a copy of your property's official survey map, or you can use graph paper or just plain paper and an architect's rule.

Incidentally, this is a great stage to involve your kids, if they are old enough. Just head out into the yard with paper, measuring tools, and a pencil. If you use graph paper, also called quadrille paper, use large 11 x 17-inch sheets or tape two 8½ x 11-inch pages together so that grids on their adjoining edges line up. Let each square on the paper equal 12 inches. Begin by drawing your property lines on the paper. Measure from your property lines to your house on all sides, and transfer those measurements to the graph paper. Then draw the house outline on the paper. Proceed in this fashion until you have included all important features of your yard on the graph paper.

Note: Also indicate obstacles and utilities, such as trees, phone and electric lines, septic system, well, and water pipes. Because you will be digging holes and setting posts, you need to avoid these obstacles. For example, you wouldn't want your Central Tower reaching near electrical wires. Also, be sure to consider the layout's relationships to entries to the house and other toy-storage buildings.

Now that you can see how much yard space is available for the play structure and its safety zones, you can begin sketching layout options.

The next step is to mark proposed outlines in the yard itself, using string and stakes.

USING AN ARCHITECT'S RULE

An architect's rule is designed for use with either plain paper or graph paper. It's a bit more complicated to use than a tape measure and graph paper, but it is more versatile. As shown, the architect's rule has three faces, which architects use to create scale versions of buildings and sites. A typical rule has 11 scales, ranging from $3/32$ inch to 1 inch, that allow you to quickly translate 1-foot units on the ground into smaller units on the scale. Thus, if you use the $1/8$-inch scale, each $1/8$ inch on paper should equal 1 foot on your yard. For most accurate results, use the largest scale that your paper size allows. Once you decide which scale to use, make a note of it on your drawing, such as "Scale $1/8$." That will remind you which scale to use when you return to the drawing. For an average-size yard, you will probably want to use 11 x 17-inch paper and either the $1/8$-inch or the $1/4$-inch scale.

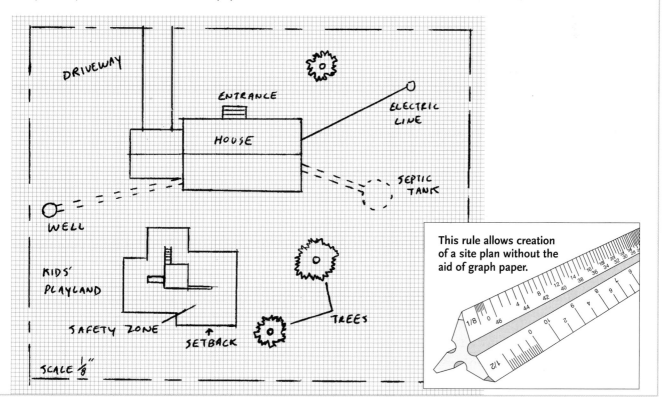

This rule allows creation of a site plan without the aid of graph paper.

LAYOUT AND FOOTPRINT OPTIONS

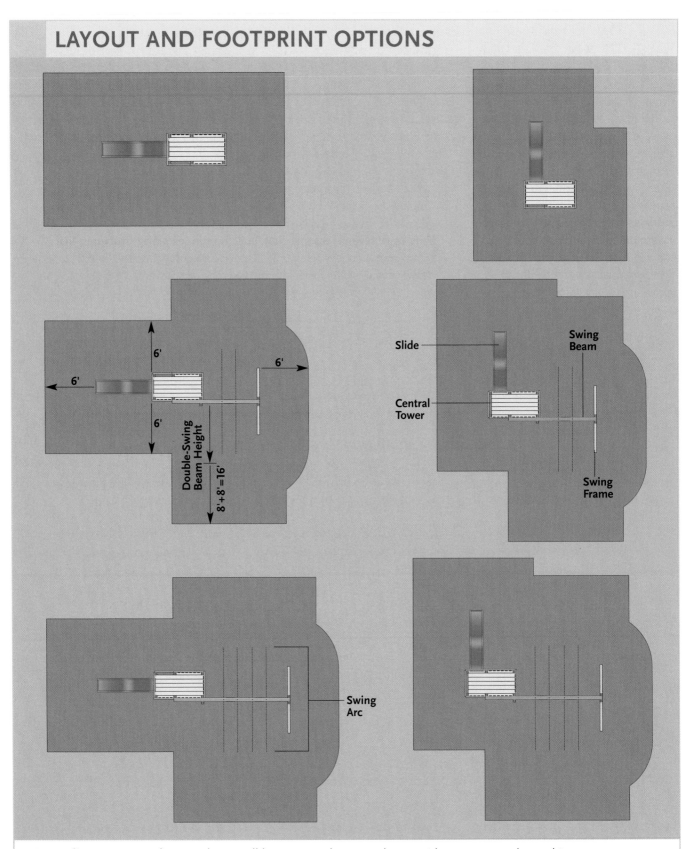

Depending on your yard space, the overall layout can take many shapes with components located in separate parts of the yard. As shown, the components can be assembled to provide different footprints. Extend impact-reducing material 6 feet from structural parts, and double the height of the swing beam.

REDUCING HAZARDS

Wherever kids are playing, accidents and injuries will occur. While you cannot build a perfectly safe play structure, you can build one that minimizes the chances of serious injury without interfering with fun.

Reducing Fall Hazards. According to the U.S. Consumer Product Safety Commission, about 60 percent of all playground injuries result from falls. And this percentage is even higher for serious injuries. Consequently, preventing falls—and minimizing their impact when they occur— should be your primary safety concern. Perhaps the best approach is to assume that children will fall off the highest point, as well as the highest point of the arc of a swing, and plan accordingly. The more resilient the surface that children land on, the less chance of injury.

Untrampled backyard grass can be a whole lot softer than schoolyard asphalt. But when kids start compacting a yard's ground surface, it can become nearly as hard as asphalt. If a child falls head first onto a grass surface from just a couple of feet, a serious injury could result. That same fall onto a surface of wood chips or pea gravel would be far less likely to cause serious injury.

To minimize danger from falls, three strategies are most useful. First, keep heights to a minimum. A high platform may be necessary to accommodate a slide or to help anchor a swing. But height is not needed for the Playhouse, where just a little elevation and some enclosure from a guardrail create all the sense of privacy and adventure that most children will need. Second, on high platforms, provide guardrails to prevent falls. Guardrails must be anchored solidly to the framing and high enough to discourage being used as a seat. Third, provide impact-reducing material where falls might occur. (See chapter 3, page 32.)

● WHY BUILD IT YOURSELF?

There are dozens of commercial play structures, especially swing sets, available in a wide range of prices. Some are inexpensive, four-legged metal swing sets that can be assembled with a few nuts and bolts in an hour or two. Others are expensive, heavy-duty wood kits that may take several weekends to assemble. With so much choice, you are certain to ask, "Why should I take the trouble to shop for assorted materials and build my own?"

There are several reasons. First, building your own play structures, like many home do-it-yourself projects, may save lots of money. Sure, you need to buy the materials, and maybe a few new tools, but the process of measuring, cutting, drilling, and assembling involve your own free labor ("sweat equity"), not someone else's.

Second, by designing and building your own structures, you will get exactly what you want. Rather than having to settle for a play set from a catalog or from store stock, you can equip your play structures with just the accessories that your kids will use and enjoy.

Third, you can build safer structures that are less likely to lead to accidents or injuries. Many people are aware that the U.S. Consumer Product Safety Commission has adopted safety standards for public playgrounds. What they may not know is that manufacturers of residential play sets are not required to comply with those standards. Recently, when a leading consumer magazine tested backyard swing sets, it found that most of them had major and minor violations of government safety recommendations. What's more, many public playgrounds are dangerous, first because many are built with little concern for safety, and second because maintenance and repairs are neglected. By following the safety guidelines and construction directions in this book, you will ensure that your structures meet or exceed safety standards for public playgrounds.

Lastly, with a little forethought, you can turn the process of designing your play structures into a family project that is both enjoyable and educational. Far from remaining passive, your kids can become active planners of a relatively large-scale, real-world activity.

Caution: We recommend that kids of most ages participate in planning and design, but we don't recommend that young kids participate in the construction itself, especially in procedures involving edged tools and power tools. Also, be sure to safeguard other construction-site hazards; this includes covering open postholes and stacking materials so that they won't invite injury.

Minimizing Chances of Collisions. Collisions are a potential hazard in any area where children move at high speed. By far, swings are the greatest hazard. You can reduce the arc, and thereby slow the velocity, of a swing by keeping its swing beam relatively low to the ground. Yet children are not likely to enjoy a "baby swing" beyond infancy.

Try to isolate the swing as much as possible from the other activities. The best strategy is to place the swing away from the rest of the play structure, but that is usually not possible on small residential lots. The kids' playland offers a compromise, with the swing a structural part of the larger unit but isolated enough to reduce chances that children will run or fall into the path of someone swinging.

Avoid placing swings too close to each other. Manufactured swing sets often space hangers of separate swings only 8 inches apart. Such tight spacing greatly heightens collision hazard. By building your own set, you can follow the much safer standards for public playgrounds, which suggest that the swings be at least 24 inches apart at about 48 inches above the level of the impact-reducing surface and be at least 30 inches from the side frame. Also, by spacing the hangers for the swing wider than the seat itself, you minimize the amount of side-to-side motion possible, further reducing the chances for collision.

If possible, place the Swing Frame next to bushes or a fence that discourages foot traffic nearby. Alternatively, you could erect a small fence that directs traffic safely around the swing. Or you could design a pathway around the swing and train the kids to use it.

The danger of a collision involving a swing is not just that the swinger's feet will kick a passing child. Even more serious are collisions with hard swing seats if a child gets too close to the swings when in use. Wood, metal, or rigid plastic seats are more likely to cause a serious injury than soft plastic or rubber seats. Soft, flexible seats are more comfortable anyway, and are usually more popular with children. They also discourage the dangerous practice of standing on the swing. For very young children, buy a commercial infant swing that provides support on all sides. Follow installation instructions.

If you decide to build swing seats from wood, make them only large enough to accommodate one child—this will help to prevent injuries. Keep any protrusions from hardware on the bottom of the seat to a minimum. A long bolt protruding from the bottom of a seat could cause serious injury if it struck a child.

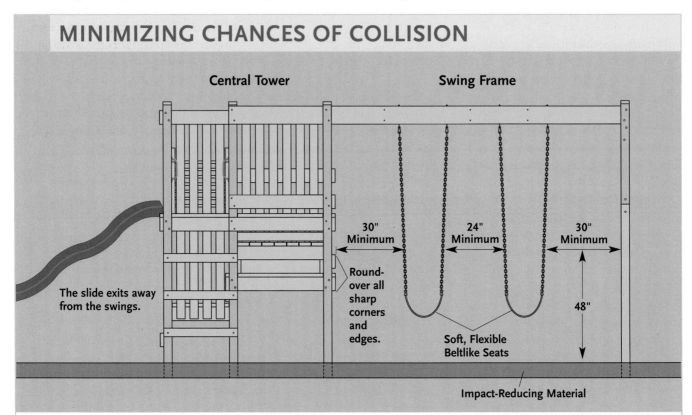

MINIMIZING CHANCES OF COLLISION

Central Tower

Swing Frame

The slide exits away from the swings.

30" Minimum

24" Minimum

30" Minimum

Round-over all sharp corners and edges.

Soft, Flexible Beltlike Seats

48"

Impact-Reducing Material

Keep the slide exit far from the swings, and keep swings a safe distance from posts and other swings. Never suspend a tire swing (which swings in all directions) next to other swings. For school-age children, use soft, flexible swing seats, as shown. For toddlers and preschoolers, see the seat options on page 44.

Preventing Head Entrapment. Wherever they find an opening, kids may try to squeeze through. An entrapped head can lead to serious injury, including strangulation. This is especially a hazard when ladders and guardrails are poorly designed. You can prevent head entrapment by keeping openings either too small for a head to fit through (that is, under 3½ inches), or too large for a head to get caught if it can pass through (that is, greater than 9 inches). If the rungs on a ladder or the risers on a stair are between 3½ and 9 inches, you should seal them up with a filler board.

Avoiding Edges, Protrusions, and Pinch Points. Corners of wood should be rounded or "softened." Also, protruding bolts can give nasty cuts and bruises, and they can snag clothing, causing falls. Avoid bolt hazards altogether by countersinking the nut end in a recess drilled in the wood, as shown below. All moving parts should be designed to eliminate pinch points. This is a particular hazard with some manufactured swing-set accessories.

Throughout this book, we've advised rounding sharp edges and eliminating protrusions and pinch points. If you make modifications that introduce related hazards, be sure to eliminate them or find a means of keeping them out of reach.

Ensuring Safer Sliding. It is possible to build a decent slide from wood and sheet metal, but we don't recommend it. Building a safe slide takes a lot of time and, in the end, won't save you any money. Today, a wide array of reasonably priced plastic slides are available. You can choose straight, wavy or curving slides, and slides with tubes that are safe, fun, and very easy to install. Chapter 3 discusses, in more depth, the choices available.

If you build or buy a metal slide, try to face it north so it won't be under direct sunlight for long periods. Otherwise, the slide may become too hot for comfort.

For any slide, you can reduce the hazard of falls by providing handholds at the entrance to support kids as they switch from standing to sitting. The

Preventing Head Entrapment. A child's head shouldn't fit into smaller gaps on the structure and should be comfortably smaller than the larger gaps.

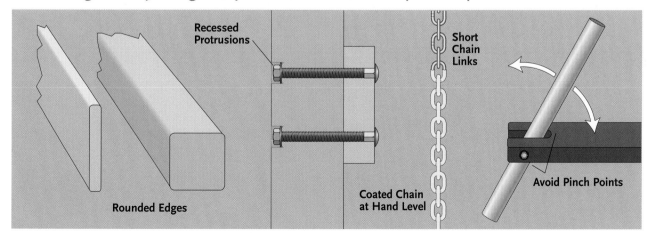

avoiding sharp edges, protrusions, and pinch points

Round-over sharp edges. Either cut off protruding bolts or recess bolts and nuts. Use chain with short links and a rubberlike plastic coating so that small fingers can't get pinched or stuck inside. Avoid commercial playground accessories, such as shown at right, with pivoting components that can pinch fingers.

slide must have continuous side rails that are 5 to 6 inches high, with top edges rounded to function as splinter-free handrails. The side rails should be integral to the chute, with no gaps between slide and rails. Slides should not descend straight to the ground. Instead, they should have a nearly horizontal exit chute that arrests the descent. A good plastic slide will meet or exceed these recommendations.

There is no ideal slide height for children of all ages. Younger children tend to be intimidated by slides more than 48 inches high, while most older children are happier with slides twice that height. A good compromise height is 60 to 72 inches. Regardless of the height, the recommended incline is about 30 degrees. Be sure to incorporate a platform at the top of the slide that allows kids to sit down before working their way onto the slide.

Likewise, the ideal drop from the exit chute to the ground varies with the size of the child. A drop of 3 to 8 inches is best for preschoolers on a short slide, while 10 to 14 inches is ideal for older children. Also, avoid any protrusions or projections at the top of the slide that could catch clothing, hands, and arms.

Careful Construction and Maintenance. Your play structures must be stable and secure. All posts should be buried in concrete to below the frost line. The top of the concrete itself should always remain below the impact-reducing material. All connections should be made with appropriate hardware, fastened securely, as shown in the construction instructions in later chapters. All parts and materials must be suitable for outdoor construction.

To be safe, a play yard needs more than just good design and construction. It also needs regular safety inspections and maintenance. Inspect all connections and surfaces on a routine basis. Tighten, fix, and replace materials and connections as needed. Replace or renew the surface of impact-reducing material when it becomes too compacted or shallow.

ENSURING SAFER SLIDING

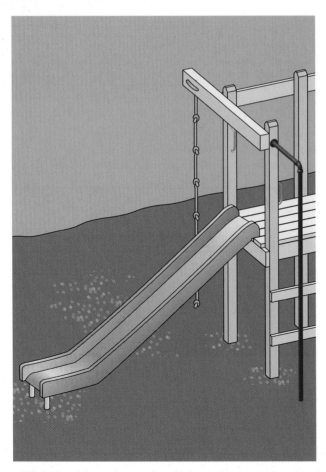

Slides should not descend straight to the ground; instead they should have landings parallel with ground level. Also ensure that no projections could catch clothing or hands. Place a metal slide so that little sun hits it.

BUILDING CODES AND PERMITS

In some jurisdictions, you will need a building permit before you begin work on an in-ground structure, such as the kids' playland. This permit is a license from local authorities to build. States and localities follow a variety of codes. Some follow one of the major national codes, and others write their own. Thus, don't assume you will be allowed to dig footings and build without a permit.

Building codes may cover height, support, materials, safety, and area covered by the structure. As part of the permit process, inspectors may need to approve construction stages, such as holes for footings as well as the finished structure. A structure found to be in violation of code can be ordered removed.

Also check your property deed before building. Your deed should show if there are easements on your property or restrictive covenants. An easement is a right-of-way granted to a utility company or other property owner that must not be blocked or otherwise restricted. A covenant can be a restriction agreed among property owners that can be enforced in court. And it's smart to check with your home insurer. These simple steps can save you a headache in the long run.

UTILITIES

Know the location of all utility lines, both underground and overhead. Water, gas, sewer, electric, or telephone lines may affect your site options.

To locate these lines, check with the customer service departments of your local utility companies. Most will help you determine the location of their service installations on your property. They might even be able to suggest ways of building over or around the service. If your house was recently built, your building inspector will probably have a copy of your hookup locations. Keep this information in your files for future reference.

If local building officials require that you obtain a construction permit, they may ask that you post it prominently. Passing inspection usually earns you a Certificate of Occupancy, often called a "C.O."

2 tools

uilding the play structures may have several long-term benefits—for example, your kids and their friends will enjoy years of outdoor fun, and they will have that fun close to home where you can keep an eye on them. But beyond that is the knowledge and confidence you will acquire in carpentry. With the experience you gain on this project, you may even consider building a deck, which involves many of the same steps. So your intentions about future projects should influence the kinds and quality of tools you purchase.

Remember, you don't need a garage full of high-priced power tools to build a play structure or tree house. In fact, you could do the entire project with few, if any, power tools. But you'll find that power tools do speed the work, especially when you tackle some of the more ambitious projects, such as the Advanced Playhouse or the Tree House.

MEASURING AND MARKING TOOLS

For the larger projects in this book, the tape measure, the chalk line, the plumb bob, and plenty of pencils are almost essential.

■ **Tape Measure.** For most of the projects, you'll find a 25- or 30-foot tape the most useful for both long and short measurements. Good tape measures have the first foot divided into $1/32$-inch increments for really precise work. Tapes with a 1-inch-wide blade are a little bulkier than $3/4$-inch blades, but 1-inch blades are much more rigid and can be extended farther without buckling. This feature is especially handy when you are working alone. When shopping for a tape, a good method for comparing options is to extend them a few inches at a time to see how far they extend before buckling. Look for a tape with a metal belt clip on the back and an easy-to-use locking mechanism.

■ **Chalk line.** Designed for marking long straight lines, a chalkline is just a roll of string inside a container filled with powdered chalk. The device allows you to mark a line between two points in a few seconds. The procedure is called "snapping a line." Here's how: stretch the line against the flat surface you want to mark. Then lift the line away from the surface and let it "snap" back. When the line hits the flat surface, chalk powder flies off, producing a straight, chalked line. Although red chalk may be easier to see, blue is a better choice because red is permanent and will stain both wood and your hands.

■ **Plumb Bob.** This heavy, pointed bob suspended from a string enables you to drop a perfectly vertical line from a given mark. For play structures, it is especially useful for aligning posts accurately. Some chalk lines can also be used as plumb bobs. Professional finish carpenters may prefer top-of-the-

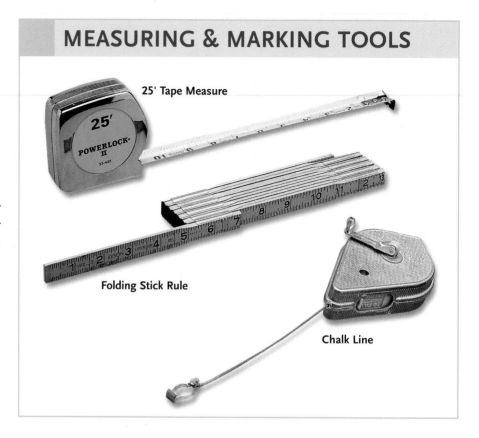

MEASURING & MARKING TOOLS

25' Tape Measure

Folding Stick Rule

Chalk Line

line plumb bobs, but for most projects a basic bob is quite adequate.

■ **Pencils.** For most marking, you will need pencils. You don't need specially manufactured wide, flat carpenter's pencils. Just have a plentiful supply of standard "lead" pencils on hand. If you later discover pencil lines you'd like to remove, sandpaper removes them quicker than an eraser.

TOOLS FOR DIGGING POSTHOLES

You'll need a shovel to remove dirt that you will replace with impact-reducing material, such as wood chips, pea gravel, or sand. You will also need a tool for digging postholes.

■ **Posthole Digger.** If you decide on projects requiring few posts or if you have time and enjoy exercise, you can dig holes by hand using a posthole digger. This double-handled tool is designed to cut deep, narrow holes and lift out dirt between its clamshell-like blades. A long, steel digging bar is

helpful in loosening the dirt and prying out rocks.

■ **Power Auger.** For quicker digging, especially requiring six or more holes, you may prefer a power auger. Powered by a gasoline engine, the power auger works like a giant drill. A hydraulic model is easier to use by one person because the engine is separate from the auger itself. Two-person units are available, with the engine mounted directly over the auger. Even if you use a power auger, you will still need a manual posthole digger to clean out the holes.

■ **Contracting for Postholes.** If you are planning to construct the entire Kids' Playland and maybe need some other holes dug too, consider hiring someone with a truck-mounted auger. Although this is the most expensive option, it can save many hours, if not days, of fairly arduous work. Check with local fence builders and landscapers for referrals.

TOOLS FOR DIGGING POSTHOLES

Shovel

Posthole Digger

2-Person Power Auger

TOOLS FOR LEVELING

Tool choices for leveling are determined by distances spanned and the degree of accuracy required.

■ **Carpenter's Level.** A must on any construction site, this tool helps you level beams and ensure that posts are plumb. Levels are available in 24- and 48-inch lengths. You don't need to spend a lot of money to get a professional-grade level, but you do need to take special care of it. One hard drop can render any level inaccurate. One way to test your level's accuracy is to set it on a level surface. The bubble or bubbles should be in the center. Next, turn the level around. The bubble or bubbles should still be in the center. On some levels the vials are ad-

justable, allowing you to correct an out-of-whack alignment. **Note:** To find level over longer spans, hold the level on a long, straight board. If necessary, secure it with tape. Using this technique, you can turn a 24-inch level into a much larger level in seconds. Spans longer than 8 feet may require the use

of a water level or a line level.

■ **Water Level.** The simplest water level is a length of $5/8$- or $5/16$-inch clear plastic tubing filled with water. You can buy the tubing by the foot at hardware stores and home centers. For the Kids' Playland, you'll need about 26 feet of tubing. With a few minutes of practice—

tools for leveling

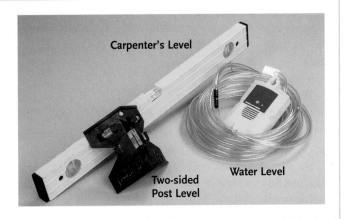

Carpenter's Level

Two-sided Post Level

Water Level

and a helper—you'll be able to transfer level lines from one post to another accurately.

■ **Line Level.** A small, inexpensive device with a single vial, a line level is designed to be hooked under a taut string to determine level over long spans. A line level isn't good for exact leveling, but for projects in this book, it is good enough. For maximum accuracy, the string needs to be taut.

TOOLS FOR SQUARING AND FINDING ANGLES

Although angles for most carpentry projects can be marked, measured, and transferred with just the framing square, smaller tools can be handier in many situations, especially for distances under 8 inches or so.

■ **Framing Square.** Sometimes called a carpenter's square or steel square, the framing square is perhaps the most commonly used marking, measuring, and squaring tool in carpentry. Its large size makes it good for marking cut lines on large boards and checking the square of lumber being joined. Made of either aluminum or steel, it usually has scales and tables that allow a variety of measurements and markings, ranging from layout of roof rafters and stair stringers to octagons.

■ **Combination Square.** The body contains both 90- and 45-degree faces and can slide up and down the blade after you unlock the thumbscrew. The movable body makes this tool ideal for transferring depth measurements or running a line along a board. Bargain-basement combination squares usually aren't worth the money. They can't be trusted to form a consistently square angle, and the dimension markings on the blade may be less than exact.

■ **Angle Square.** A thick, strong, triangular casting of either aluminum or plastic makes this square tough enough

to withstand the rigors of general construction without losing its accuracy. The angle square's triangular shape enables you to lay out a 45-degree angle as quickly as a 90-degree angle. Using markings on the body, you can lay out angles other than 90 degrees, as when laying out rafters. The edges of the square can also serve when setting 90- and 45-degree blade angles on a circular saw.

■ **Bevel Gauge.** Probably the best tool for gauging and transferring angles other than 45 and 90 degrees is a sliding bevel gauge, also known as a T-bevel. This device has a flat sliding metal blade that can be locked into the handle at any angle. A bevel gauge is great for transferring an existing angle on the actual project. It can also be used along with a protractor to record and transfer a specific angle.

WOOD-CUTTING TOOLS

Most people rank cutting and joining among the most enjoyable aspects of carpentry. This results, at least in part, from the feeling of accomplishment that accompanies working with wood and making it fit the intended design. And enjoyment can be enhanced if you have the proper tools. More important, having the right tool for a specific job and knowing how to use it are the best ways to avoid wasting material and preventing injuries.

■ **Circular Saw.** On our play structures, a circular saw is perfectly adequate for cutting lumber. For most do-it-yourselfers, the circular saw has replaced the hand saw in almost every situation. That's because a circular saw is capable of crosscutting, ripping, and

SQUARING AND ANGLE TOOLS

Speed Square

Bevel Gauge

Try Square

Framing Square

Combination Square

Small Square

beveling boards or sheets of plywood quickly and cleanly. This multipurpose saw can also be used to create a variety of joints, such as miters, laps, and dadoes.

The circular saws most popular with carpenters and do-it-yourselfers alike are models that take a blade of 7¼-inch diameter. This blade size allows cuts to a maximum depth of about 2½ inches at 90 degrees. This saw also allows you to cut off 4x4 posts, simply by making two cuts, one each on opposing sides.

Choosing a Circular Saw. Several features distinguish circular saws. Perhaps the most important is power. One of the best gauges of a saw's potential performance is the amount of amperage its motor draws, not merely the saw's horsepower. Low-cost saws may have only 9- to 11-amp motors with drive shafts and arbors running on rollers or sleeve bearings. A contractor-grade saw is rated at 12 to 15 amps and is made with ball bearings. The extra power and the bearings enable the saw to withstand wear better, especially when cutting tough, pressure-treated lumber. Top-of-the-line models are intended for heavy, daily use by professional carpenters. Midrange saws lack some of the power and durability of the best saws, but they still cut easier and cleaner (and thus more safely) than low-cost saws.

Plastic housings are no longer the mark of an inferior saw, but a thin, stamped-metal base is. A thicker base, extruded or cast, will stay flatter longer.

Your saw should be double insulated to minimize any chance of electric shock. Some saws have an additional safety switch that must be depressed before the trigger will work. Another feature to look for is an arbor lock. The lock secures the arbor nut and prevents the blade from turning while you are changing the blade. A blade brake is a highly desirable safety feature. The brake stops the blade from spinning almost the moment you release the trigger. **Note:** A saw with a special port for dust-collection can be useful indoors.

Choosing Circular-Saw Blades. For general use, carbide-tipped blades are the best for achieving smooth, precise cuts. Carbide blades cost more than blades made from high-speed steel, but they can also cut much longer before needing to be sharpened.

Saw-blade manufacturers offer a wide variety of blades. You can choose blades specifically made to cut plywood, two-by framing lumber, pressure-treated lumber, or one-by pine.

WOOD-CUTTING TOOLS

Circular Saw

Saber Saw

Sliding Compound Miter Saw

Hand Miter Saw

Power Miter Saw

Trim Blade

Block Plane

A blade with fewer than 30 teeth will cut quicker but leave a rougher surface, while a 40- to 60-tooth blade is better for smooth cuts, especially when cross-cutting (cutting across the grain). Blades are also made especially for ripping with the grain.

The key to choosing the right blade is knowing what kind of cutting you will do. A good choice for the do-it-yourselfer who wants to buy only one blade is a combination, or general-purpose, blade. This blade will do an adequate job crosscutting and ripping most wood products. But if you plan to use the blade primarily to crosscut lumber, you might be happier using a blade made especially for crosscutting. It's easy to change a blade in a circular saw, and blades aren't very expensive. So don't be afraid to buy several special-purpose blades and change them as needed.

A good blade collection would include a ripping, a combination, and a finishing blade. Newer generation thin-kerf blades keep improving. They cut faster and place less stress on the saw motor and gearing. You can also buy blades designed to cut masonry, metal, and ceramics, though you won't need them for any of the play structures.

■ **Larger Saws.** For quicker and more accurate cuts than you can get with a circular saw, you might consider a table saw, a radial arm saw, or a power miter saw (commonly referred to as a chop saw). Each can quickly and accurately crosscut lumber and can also cut dadoes, bevels, and miters. The table saw is the most versatile for ripping, especially sheet material such as plywood. For mitering small pieces of wood, a simple miter box and hand saw are perfectly adequate.

■ **Saber Saw.** Also called a jigsaw or bayonet saw, a saber saw is a good tool for cutting curves, cutouts, or other elaborate shapes. Shop for a saber saw with variable speed, a thick baseplate, and at least a 3$\frac{1}{2}$-amp motor. Bimetal blades provide the best service and last the longest.

■ **Hand Saw.** For some cuts, no power saw can completely replace a good hand saw. In fact, a hand saw is often quicker when you have just a couple of cuts to make, or for tough-to-reach spots. A 15-inch saw with 10 to 12 teeth per inch (tpi) will cut well and still fit into a toolbox.

■ **Plane.** A properly set plane will quickly trim a board for a better fit. You can also use it to chamfer, or "soften," the edges on a board.

■ **Chisels.** A set of three or four chisels, from $\frac{1}{4}$ to 1$\frac{1}{2}$ inches wide, will also be useful for close paring. To work safely and smoothly, the blades must be kept sharp.

DRILLING TOOLS

For these projects, a drill is absolutely indispensable.

■ **Hand Drill and Hand Brace.** For holes up to $\frac{1}{4}$ inch in diameter and up to 1 or 2 inches in depth, you could get by using a hand drill and bits. Besides, a smaller manual drill and bits allow you to drill pilot holes for screws. A hand brace and a few large-diameter bits would be sufficient for bolt holes.

■ **Power Drill.** For quicker results, you will need an electric drill. The best choice for most do-it-yourselfers is a drill with a $\frac{3}{8}$-inch chuck, a variable speed control, and a reversing switch. A keyless chuck is a great convenience. If you're willing to spend a little more money, you should seriously consider buying a cordless drill. The quality of cordless drills has improved dramatically, and the selection is huge. For do-it-yourselfers, a drill powered by a 9.6 or 12-volt battery will suffice. A cordless drill equipped with an adjustable clutch allows you to drive screws safely, without burying the heads deeper than you intended. On many models, the battery will recharge in just 10 to 15 minutes.

■ **Drill Bits.** Standard drill-bit sets are available in sizes from $\frac{1}{16}$ to $\frac{1}{4}$ inch, and a set of wood-boring (spade) bits allow you to drill holes up to 1 inch or more. Other accessories allow you to convert your power drill into a grinder, sander, or paint stirrer.

DRILLING TOOLS

Cordless Drill

Drill Bit Set

SAFETY EQUIPMENT

Many thousands of do-it-yourselfers are injured every year while using hand and power tools, often because they failed to use basic safety equipment, especially eye and ear protection.

■ **Eye Protectors.** Wear safety goggles and plastic glasses whenever you are working with power tools. Also wear goggles whenever working with chemicals. Make sure that your eye protection conforms with American National Standards Institute (ANSI) or Canadian Standards Association (CSA) requirements. Considering the cost of a visit to the emergency room and possible permanent injury, safety gear is a small investment. And it doesn't hurt to have an extra pair of eye or hearing protectors for the times when a neighbor volunteers to help or if your first pair becomes misplaced.

■ **Hearing Protectors.** The U.S. Occupational Safety and Health Administration (OSHA) recommends that hearing protection be worn when the noise level equals or exceeds an 8-hour average of 85 decibels (db). Because many power tools emit more than 85 db when operated, it's best to err on the side of caution. Hearing protectors are available as muffs and as earplugs. Whichever style you choose, look for a noise reduction rating (NRR) of at least 20 db.

■ **Dust Masks.** Your construction project will create a lot of sawdust. If you are sensitive to dust, and especially if you are working with pressure-treated wood, it's important to wear a dust mask approved for protection from the National Institute for Occupational Safety and Health and the Mine Safety and Health Administration (NIOSH/MSHA). Replace the dust mask with a new one regularly.

■ **Hand and Foot Protectors.** Work gloves help avoid injury to the hands—catching a splinter off a board or developing a blister when digging postholes can spoil a workday. Heavy-duty work boots will help protect your feet. Steel toes will prevent injuries from dropped boards or tools. Flexible steel soles will protect your feet from puncture by a rogue nail.

■ **Clothing and Grooming.** At a construction site, attire and grooming can greatly determine safety. Avoid loose clothing and jewelry that can catch on boards, tools, and hardware. Also, tie back long hair.

■ **Shock Protector.** Power tools should be plugged into a receptacle equipped with a ground-fault circuit interrupter (GFCI). A GFCI helps prevent electric shocks from faulty tools or extension cords. In other words, it can save a life. If a GFCI receptacle isn't available, use a GFCI-equipped extension cord. And before operating any power tool, check the cord and plug carefully. If either is damaged, have it replaced by a qualified service center or get a new GFCI.

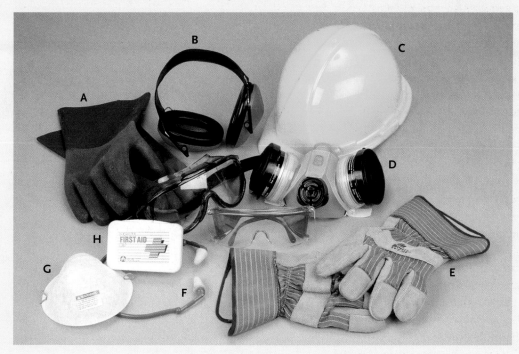

A—rubber gloves
B—ear protectors
C—hard hat
D—filtered respirator
E—work gloves
F—ear plugs
G—dust mask
H—first-aid kit

SANDING TOOLS

■ **Hand Sanders.** For play-yard projects, you can get by using a plentiful supply of sandpaper and a good sanding block. Coarse- to medium-grit sandpaper (40 to 80 grit) will handle most of the work. Also, a rasp-cut file or surface-forming tool is handy for quickly smoothing rough edges.

■ **Power Sander.** A belt sander would be the best power sander for projects here because it can round-over edges and smooth boards with just a couple of quick passes. **Note:** Belt sanders can remove a lot of wood very quickly, so they can be tricky to operate well. Read the owner's manual carefully and practice on scrap lumber before tackling the real thing.

THE ROUTER

You won't need a router and bits just to build a play structure. But if you've been planning to buy a router anyway, it will be handy for rounding edges on the structure.

Most veteran woodworkers feel their router is about the most important and versatile tool in their shop. A router can shape edges, cut grooves, and shape molding. A router with a fixed base will be adequate for occasional and uncomplicated use. But a good-quality plunge router is much more versatile. The motor on a plunge router is attached to two rods that allow it to slide up and down in relation to the base. This feature allows you to plunge the bit into the middle of a workpiece, which can't be done using a fixed-base router. This also allows you to adjust depth stops in order to make a deep cut in a series of successively deeper passes.

When choosing a router, you must also decide on the size of collet, which is the small part that holds the bit.

Router, Guide, and Bits

Routers with ¼-inch collets are less expensive and can be satisfactory for small tasks and infrequent use. But a model with a ½-inch collet will hold larger bits and perform tougher work.

Router bits are available in dozens of shapes. On this project, a chamfer and a roundover bit will come in handy for "softening" the edges. Like saw blades, router bits with a carbide-tipped edges will stay sharp longer, though high-speed steel will cost less.

SANDING TOOLS

Surform Tool

Belt Sander

Mini Files

Large Files

File Card

OTHER TOOLS

This category covers the range of tools that any do-it-yourselfer should have in the toolbox.

■ **Turn Fasteners.** It's nearly mandatory to have a full complement of screwdrivers, wrenches, and pliers. A ³/₈-inch socket wrench and a set of sockets will allow you to quickly tighten nuts and drive lag screws.

■ **Hammers.** You should have a standard curved-claw hammer weighing at least 16 ounces. A lighter hammer may be helpful for fastening small pieces and driving small nails. If you'll be driving a lot of 12d or 16d nails, you will quickly learn to appreciate the greater ease and driving power of a 20- or 22-ounce framing hammer. (In most cases, we've instead recommended deck screws as the prime fasteners. They're easier to drive, using a cordless electric drill driver, and far easier to remove during disassembly.)

■ **Nail Sets.** These complement a hammer. A nail set is a punch-shaped shaft designed to countersink finishing nails or to drive them flush with the wood surface without marring the wood with unsightly hammer "dings." The points of nail sets come in various diameters approximating nailhead sizes. The point may even be cupped to secure the nailhead during driving. For best results, use a point about the size of the nailhead. Countersunk holes can be filled with wood putty to produce a finish that looks nail free.

■ **Clamps.** Several large C-clamps, bar clamps, or hand-squeezed spring clamps will help hold boards and posts together while you drill bolt holes.

■ **Bolt-Cutting Tools.** You may also need a hacksaw or bolt cutter to shorten bolts so you can recess them. This will avoid protrusions that can become hazards.

■ **Utility Knife.** Well named, this knife can be used for a wide range of tasks—from sharpening pencils to marking lines, from opening boxes to shaving wood. For general use, invest in a fairly heavy-duty model that has a large retractable blade. As with all cutting tools, sharp blades are safest because they provide the most control with the least amount of effort. Replacement blades are inexpensive, yet they can also be sharpened quickly with a few passes on a whetstone.

■ **Tool Holders.** Unless you enjoy hunting for misplaced tools, a tool belt or work apron is a must. A good tool belt will have holders for a hammer, tape measure, chalkline, pencil, and other commonly used tools, as well as pouches for generous supplies of nails or screws.

■ **Work Surface.** At the very least, you will need a couple of sawhorses. A workbench may also come in handy. You can create a temporary, and portable, workbench by laying a sheet of ³/₄-inch plywood onto two sawhorses. Cut the plywood to the size that suits you.

OTHER TOOLS

Hammer and Nail Sets

Utility Knife

Spring Clamp

C-Clamp

Lightweight Bar Clamp

Quick-release Clamp

3 materials

Many elements will play a part in your choice of materials for your backyard project, including cost, appearance, safety considerations, and how well the material will stand up to the abuse inflicted by the kids playing on the structure. When shopping and comparing prices, remember that a cheaper product may save some money at first but will be more expensive in the total scheme of things if it is unsafe.

All of the projects in this book are made from wood, but other materials play an equally important part, such as concrete, swing-set hardware, and accessories such as slides. You will also need to select materials that make the swing and play area safe should someone fall. These include impact-reducing materials that cushion falls. There are a number available, including sand, wood chips, and gravel.

WOOD

The wood in a play structure must fulfill these requirements: it must survive years of exposure without losing its strength or stability. It must also resist the combined effects of sun, rain, mold, and wood-boring insects. In addition, the wood should be easy to work, attractive, and affordable.

Finding appropriate wood isn't difficult. Lumber is divided into two main categories: softwoods and hardwoods. Softwoods come from coniferous trees, often called evergreens. And hardwoods come from broad-leaved deciduous trees that lose their leaves in the winter. While most hardwoods are harder than most softwoods, there are exceptions. For example, southern yellow pine, a softwood, is harder than poplar, a hardwood.

Today, nearly all outdoor construction is done with softwoods because they are more readily available than hardwoods, easier to work with, and generally less expensive. Softwoods are the woods used for pressure treating with preservatives. Of the softwoods, redwood, cedar, and cypress are considered the most desirable for outdoor building because of their beauty and natural resistance to decay. These woods are used on decks, gazebos, and siding, and for shingles and shakes. But because these woods are in limited supply, they are the most expensive softwoods, and they may not be available in all regions of North America.

You don't need to use high-priced redwood or cedar to create an attractive play structure. Besides, in the event your play structure will be temporary, the more expensive softwoods may be more than you need. Other softwoods—including pine, fir, spruce, and larch—are widely available and more affordable. While these woods require additional weather protection, they can give many years of reliable

service, and they look good.

Wood is prized for its durability and structural capabilities. It has high resistance to impact and high strength in compression relative to its weight. And it can easily be formed into many shapes without seriously altering its structural characteristics. However, wood often has natural defects that can weaken it, such as knots, splits, and checks. It can also suffer shrinkage, decay, and warping. And different species of wood may have quite different characteristics.

The availability of particular wood

species depends to some extent on geographical location, and prices can vary over time and from region to region. Wood officially becomes lumber after it has been sawn and planed to standard sizes and graded by characteristics guaranteed by the manufacturer. This guarantee of size, strength, and other characteristics assures you that the wood will behave in a predictable manner.

As far as price and availability go, the best advice is to shop around, and ask questions. Most home centers and lumberyards have at least a few sales-

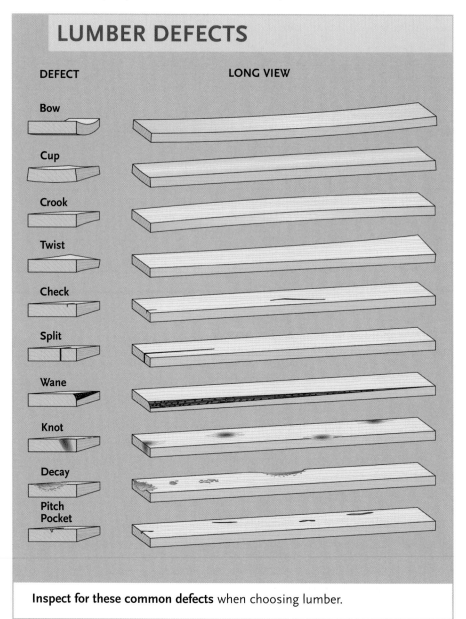

LUMBER DEFECTS

DEFECT	LONG VIEW
Bow	
Cup	
Crook	
Twist	
Check	
Split	
Wane	
Knot	
Decay	
Pitch Pocket	

Inspect for these common defects when choosing lumber.

people with building experience or who otherwise have good knowledge of building supplies.

■ **Redwood.** The redwood trees of the Pacific Northwest are legendary for their size and lumber quality. Redwood's beautiful straight grain, natural glowing color, and weather resistance have traditionally made it the premier wood for outdoor building. Unfortunately, over harvesting has reduced redwood availability and driven up its price.

As in all logs, the redwood's younger, outer portion is called sapwood. The older, denser center is called heartwood. Sapwood is lighter in color and less weather resistant than heartwood. Redwood heartwood is extremely stable and can be milled to produce very smooth surfaces. When sawn, the reddish heartwood produces a wonderful fragrance by releasing the same chemicals that discourage wood-boring insects. If you like, you can let redwood age naturally to a light gray patina. It will readily accept paint or stain.

There are several grades of redwood. The two grades preferred for outdoor construction, because they consist entirely of heartwood, are Clear All Heart and Construction Heart. Of the two, Clear All Heart is more expensive because it is knot free. On a play structure, the high price of Clear All Heart tends to limit its use to railings, if used at all. In comparison, Construction Heart (Con-Heart) contains minor imperfections but is ideal for almost every other element of a play structure. Although they contain some sapwood, Clear, B Grade, Construction Common, Deck Common, and Merchantable grades of redwood are all suitable for smaller accessories in your play structure.

Although it is weather and rot resistant, when in contact with the ground, redwood does not last as long as pressure-treated lumber, nor would it be as strong in stress if used as posts for the swing beam. For these reasons, if you want to use mostly redwood, we recommend substituting pressure-treated lumber for the posts and parts of any other projects in contact with the ground.

■ **Cedar.** The heartwood of all types of cedar has better-than-average resistance to decay. Like redwood, western red cedar is a fragrant, dark-colored wood that is extremely stable and rot resistant. It can be left to age to a gray patina, or it can be stained or painted. Cedar does have drawbacks. It is softer and weaker than other species; cedar is not recommended for the framing members. Its price is high because its a popular choice for cedar shingles, clapboards, and shakes, limiting its availability.

■ **Cypress.** Baldcypress, often called "cypress," is the South's answer to redwood. Native to the swamps and lowland areas throughout the Southeast, cypress is extremely resistant to decay and insect attack. Cypress is similar to redwood in hardness and strength, although it's not as stable. In the southern United States, local sawmills can be economical sources of cypress. Although cypress isn't usually stocked outside its native region, you may be able to order it if you live elsewhere.

■ **Other Decay-Resistant Woods.** Depending on where you live, you may have access to local wood species with heartwood that is quite resistant to rot. Osage orange, black locust, and white oak are all potentially good choices for outdoor projects. Most of these species will not be readily available through home centers, so you'll need to inquire with local sawmills, and conduct your own surfacing and drying.

GRADES OF REDWOOD

Grades with Only Heartwood	Grades with Some Sapwood	Characteristics
Clear All Heart	Clear	Essentially knot-free
B Heart	B Grade	Limited knots
Construction Heart	Construction Common	Knottier than B
Deck Heart	Deck Common	Graded specifically for strength; similar to construction grades
Merchantable Heart	Merchantable	Larger knots and knotholes

Source: California Redwood Association

life expectancy of wood in contact with the ground

Southern yellow pine
Treated	42 years
Untreated	3–12 years

Western red cedar   8–24 years

Redwood   20 years

Source: U.S. Forest Products Laboratory

ROPE

Chain is a better choice than rope for suspending swings primarily because it can be used with durable and safe fittings. Rope must be tied to beams and seats, with weaker and less durable connections. Yet rope is good for climbing. Simply loop a few knots along its length to provide hand holds and suspend it from a beam.

When buying rope, you can choose between natural fiber and synthetics. High-grade manila hemp (abaca) is good for play structures, especially for climbing. It's strong and less abrasive on hands than other types, and not nearly as slippery. Because it is popular with boaters, boatyards can be a source.

Synthetic rope is strong, but slippery. It is better for supporting swings than for climbing. Avoid polypropylene because it does not hold up well to the sun and cold. Of the synthetic ropes, polyethylene rope is probably the best choice, although nylon is nearly as good.

Be sure to check the rope manufacturer's label for the maximum load that the rope is intended to support. One-half inch nylon or polyethylene is plenty strong for our Swing Frame. If you use polypropylene, which is much weaker, you will need to at least double the thickness to support the same amount of weight.

PLAY ACCESSORIES

You can choose from among many dozens of manufactured accessories. This allows you to customize your project to meet your needs, and it offers the opportunity to add new accessories as your children tire of or outgrow the original activities.

To find the broadest selection, be prepared to shop around. Toy and department stores may offer a small selection, home centers a little more. Also check with playground experts at local schools and parks, and consult telephone Yellow Pages under playground-related headings. Some of the largest selections may be available through mail order. The following section surveys some of the options.

■ **Swings.** Swing seats for babies and infants are usually bucket-style, made of rigid plastic or wood. They should either be fully enclosed, making it impossible for the child to slip out or climb out, or be equipped with a child-proof safety strap. In addition to design features, safe use requires constant adult presence.

Adult-supervised toddlers are comfortable in soft-rubber or molded plastic half-bucket seats that provide support to the lower back and may also include a safety strap.

For older kids, the choices are more numerous. Most older kids are happy with a flexible belt-style seat, which

may be made of soft rubber, canvas, or plastic. You can also choose flat, rigid seats made from wood, rubber, or plastic. As mentioned earlier, hard seats increase the hazard of injury in the event the seat strikes another child.

Some swings, especially those for the youngest children, are sold with rope or chain already attached. You should be able to find swing seats in a variety of colors.

■ **Slides.** The most commonly available slides are 8 and 10 feet long, made of molded polyethylene, in a choice of colors. You can choose straight or wavy models (the latter will slide a bit slower). These slides can be attached to a platform deck in a matter of minutes with just a couple of screws. Heavy-duty models are thicker and may be reinforced with side rails.

Most kids seem to love tube slides, which can be straight or twisting. But tube slides have disadvantages. They cost considerably more than standard slides, and they are more complicated to install. Also, from standpoints of safety and parental supervision, tubes conceal children inside and somewhat obscure the view behind them. In addition, twisting tubes may prevent the second child's ability to see when a previous child has cleared the tube and stepped safely away from the landing.

All slides are manufactured to be installed on decks of a specified height,

swing seats

Full bucket is safest for toddlers.

Half bucket is good for preschoolers.

Belt seat is one of the safest for school-age kids.

Rigid seat could encourage unsafe standing and is hard upon impact.

SLIDES

Wave slide of molded polyethylene

TIRE-SWING CONNECTORS

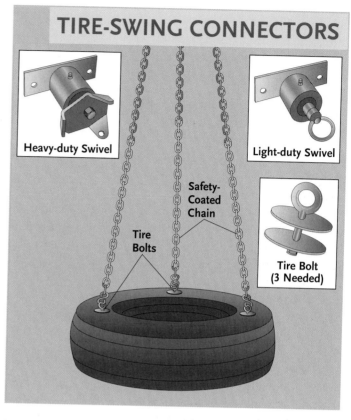

Heavy-duty Swivel

Light-duty Swivel

Safety-Coated Chain

Tire Bolts

Tire Bolt (3 Needed)

gymnastic equipment

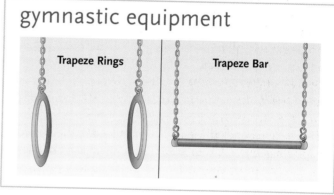

Trapeze Rings

Trapeze Bar

---

usually 48 to 60 inches. It's vital to match your slide to deck height.

■ **Gymnastic Equipment.** In place of a permanent or temporary swing, you may want to hang a trapeze bar, with or without a set of rings attached. Spring-loaded connector clips allow you to switch gymnastic accessories in a couple of minutes. Also, instead of the Monkey Bar we've designed for the Kids' Playland, your kids might prefer trapeze rings.

■ **Other Swings.** Tire swings are popular, especially because they can be used by two or three children at once.

Tire swings can be hung from the main swing beam. But avoid installing a tire swing near another swing. Because it swings in all directions, a tire swing would be likely to collide with nearby swings. You can buy tire swings complete or buy special hardware that allows you to convert your own spare tire into a swing. Tire swings should be installed with tire-swivel hardware, following the manufacturer's instructions. Also, several variations on the tire swing offer a similar type of swinging movement, but for only one child at a time.

Caution: Don't use steel-belted radial tires because exposed belting on worn tires can be sharp.

Other possibilities include swing discs and ball swings, often preferred by older children.

■ **Swing Hardware.** You'll need tire swivels to install a tire swing. Manufacturers also offer specialized swing hangers, at modest cost, that can speed installation. Hangers are available with a threaded screw or machine thread that requires a nut and washer. However, assemblies with only one threaded screw lack heavy-duty strength.

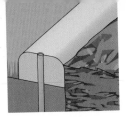

4 techniques

Every carpenter develops unique approaches to construction projects. Yet if you were to watch a group of pros, you would notice similarities in the ways they perform many tasks. Of course, you can learn by trial and error in the school of hard knocks, but you don't need to learn everything that way.

This chapter provides a foundation of basic techniques. And it will help you build play structures correctly on the first try, with a minimum of wasted time and materials. As a bonus, you'll find that most of the skills transfer to other projects, particularly other outdoor structures, such as fences and decks. Although there are tricks of the trade, good building skills are basically common sense applied to shapes, materials, tools, and techniques.

Let commonsense principles guide your work. Take your time; work safely; and never forget the carpenter's creed: "Measure twice, cut once."

SETTING UP THE WORK SITE

Good carpenters heed the Shaker motto "a place for everything and everything in its place." If you've done some building, you may recall having wasted time looking for misplaced tools, climbing over stacked lumber, moving materials about, misplacing tools, and making extra trips to purchase forgotten items. If you've known such inefficiencies, you'll better appreciate how even a small project can devour an entire weekend. This book will help you plan better. Besides, a well-planned work site is a lot safer.

Often a quick sketch of the work site helps you visualize how the work should flow. In your sketch, try to include all the major construction elements: where the wood will be delivered, how the car or truck will reach delivery points with minimal damage to lawn or garden, where electrical cords will run, where you will perform most of the cutting, and so on. Try to imagine how these factors will relate. Then plan the work site accordingly. For example, if you will deliver lumber yourself, unload near enough to the proposed play structure to minimize wood toting but distant enough to keep materials out of your way when you begin work. If you plan to have a bulldozer remove the sod or a truck-mounted auger drill the postholes, sketch paths for the vehicles. It's also wise to have most power tools in one general location. This helps minimize the moving of sawhorses, for example, and it isolates the tripping hazard of power cords.

Besides your time in this project, your biggest investment will be in the wood. To avoid unnecessary damage to the wood and injury to yourself, use a little forethought before you stack the wood. For example, the weight from a properly stacked pile will prevent boards from cupping and warping. Also decide how and where you will pile wood scraps so they don't get in the way. Upon delivery of the lumber, begin sorting it by best and worst pieces; that way you'll know which piles or portions of piles to use for visible and hidden portions of the project. If the lumber will be stored outdoors, apply a rain cover that first day to protect the material from the weather.

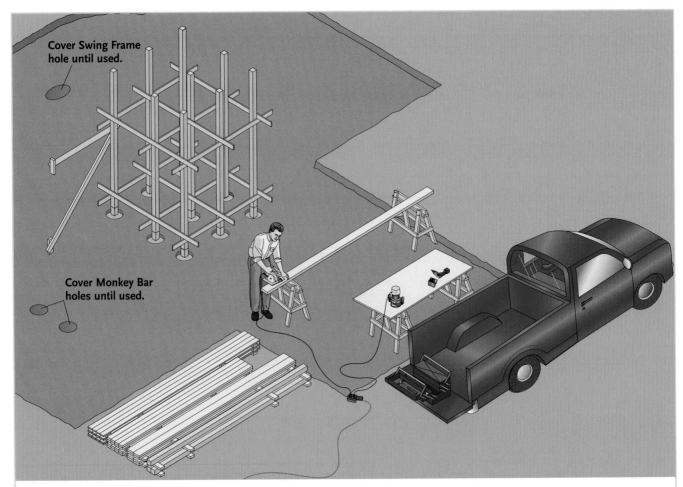

Cover Swing Frame hole until used.

Cover Monkey Bar holes until used.

Setting Up the Work Site. In an efficient work site, tools and materials are placed strategically to save footsteps, allow working room, and promote safety. Note that the lumber is stacked to allow convenient end-of-stack removal.

PREPARING THE SITE

Site preparation involves some of the most important decisions on the project. What kind of impact-reducing material will you use? How deep do you want it? Will the surface be at grade (ground level) or above grade? Your answers will be affected by desired appearance, as well as costs in time and dollars. Here are several options:

■ **An Above-Grade Surface.** The simplest approach is to place the surface above grade. This allows you to build on top of the lawn, without the hassle of first removing sod and topsoil before adding a border and filling in with impact-reducing material. Note that the border should be high enough to hold the depth of material required. (See the table "Impact-Reducing Materials" on page 40). You may find it necessary to remove the turf and level the area to ensure the proper depth of impact-reducing material.

Because this border will be a step up from grade, it must be strong and solid. For this, you can use pressure-treated 4x6s or landscape timbers. The top edges of the timbers should be smooth and rounded. (Landscape timbers are normally sold with two rounded edges.) To hold the border in place, drill holes through the timbers about every 48 inches. Then use a sledgehammer to drive 18- to 20-inch lengths of steel reinforcing bar, called rebar, through the holes into the ground. Be sure to drive the rebar below the top surface of the timber so that it doesn't protrude.

To ensure that grass and weeds won't grow through the edge materials, install landscape fabric. This fabric is preferable to polyethylene sheeting because it allows water to drain through. Finally, fill the enclosure with at least 6 inches of wood mulch or wood chips, or with the appropriate depth of sand or pea gravel.

● SAWHORSES

On a work site, few devices are more useful than a pair of good sawhorses. First, they offer a sturdy, safe surface on which to measure, mark, and cut lumber. Second, they become part of a workbench when you lay a sheet of plywood over them.

Some carpenters build elaborate sawhorses, which they pamper and carry from job to job. Others see sawhorses as temporary supports, best built in minutes from scrap lumber on site and then torn apart when the job is done. The choice is yours.

The sawhorse shown without bracing can be built in about ten minutes and requires only three materials: 2x4s, 1x6s, and either 10d nails or 3-inch screws. Begin by cutting an 8-foot 2x4 in half to serve as the top of the horse. Then fasten the two pieces in an inverted T, as shown. Cut legs from the 1x6 to the length you prefer; 30 to 36 inches suits most people. Then attach each leg to each 2x4 with either nails or screws. If the sawhorses will support heavy loads, such as a long 4x6 beam, add 1x4 bracing to the legs. When you finish your play structures, you can either store the sawhorses or tear them apart.

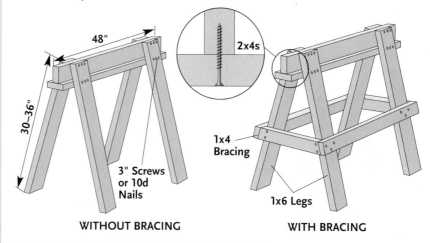

WITHOUT BRACING   WITH BRACING

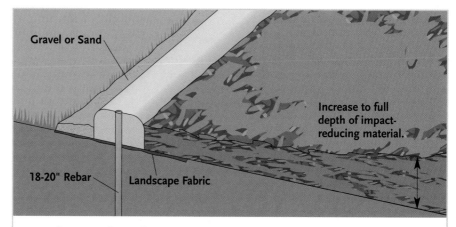

An Above-Grade Surface. Install lumber or timbers to enclose impact-reducing materials. Round-over edges and corners of timbers.

surfacing options

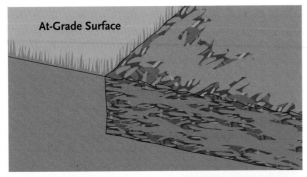

At-Grade Surface

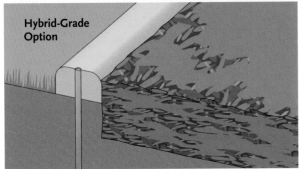

Hybrid-Grade Option

An at-grade surface requires more work than an above-grade surface but reduces tripping hazards along the border and helps make the play areas look better integrated. A good compromise is to place the impact-reducing material partly above and partly below grade.

LAYING OUT THE SITE

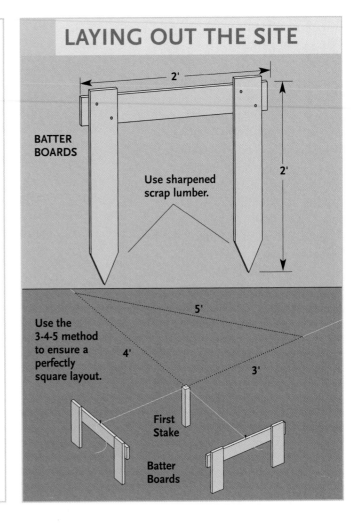

2'

BATTER BOARDS

Use sharpened scrap lumber.

2'

Use the 3-4-5 method to ensure a perfectly square layout.

5'

4'

3'

First Stake

Batter Boards

■ **An At-Grade Surface.** An at-grade surface blends with the yard better than an above-grade surface. But it involves considerably more work. To set the surface at grade, you will need to excavate to the depth your surface material will fill (6 to 10 inches). While you could excavate by hand, you may be better off hiring a contractor with a bulldozer. If you decide to do your own digging, consider renting a rototiller to loosen the soil. A heavy-duty tiller will reach down as far as 12 inches, making digging and removal much easier. But first, you might want to carefully dig up the sod and install it elsewhere in your yard. Or dig it up before rototilling and mix it with your compost.

With the hole dug, you can line the edges with landscape fabric, available at garden suppliers. After building the play structure, fill the excavated area

with the impact-reducing material of your choice.

■ **Hybrid-Grade Option.** You could borrow a little from each of the two grade approaches above by building a slightly raised border. For example, you could use 3x5 landscape timbers; then remove only the sod and perhaps a couple of inches of topsoil. This hybrid approach allows you to reach a depth of at least 6 inches, the minimum for safety, without needing to do extensive excavation.

LAYING OUT THE SITE

Site layout establishes precise locations for the posts. Once set, the posts become reference points for all remaining construction.

In this book, you'll find many op-

tional layouts for the play structure. And although the dimensions between posts in the drawing are suggested, you may wish to alter them. Either way, it's important to understand the principles of layout described here.

The main tools of layout are a tape measure, batter boards, string, and a plumb bob. To make square corners, it's helpful to understand mathematical relationships expressed in the Pythagorean theorem, but not absolutely necessary. The theorem states that the squares (side x itself) of the lengths of the two short sides of a right triangle will always equal the square of the length of the long side ($a^2 + b^2 = c^2$). On the work site, it may be easier just to remember and apply the theorem as the 3-4-5 rule, as shown in accompanying illustrations. That is, the intersections of the string lines (which

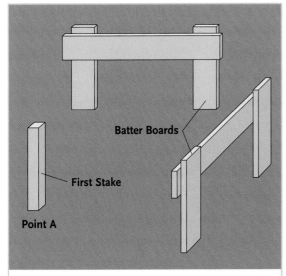

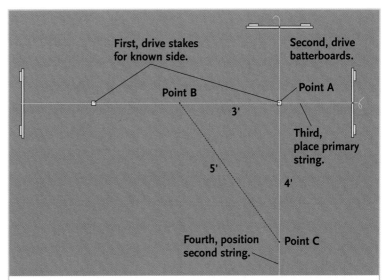

1 **Drive stakes** at the approximate corners of the structure. Then erect batter boards.

2 **After driving the two stakes** and batter boards for the known side of the structure, use intersecting strings to determine post positions.

will become the corners of the structure) will be perfectly square when the diagonal distance from the 3-foot location on one line and the 4-foot location on the other equals 5 feet. That is because 3^2 (or 9) + 4^2 (or 16) = 5^2 (or 25). This principle also holds true for any multiple of 3-4-5, such as 6-8-10 or 9-12-15.

1 **Find Rough Dimensions.** Decide where you want one side of the play structure to be (usually the side nearest the house). Drive two small stakes where you would like its corner posts. Placement of these two stakes is important, because they become the two corner references for the entire layout.

Erect batter boards at approximate right angles to each other about 2 feet outside the stake at Point A. Erect a second batter board outside the second stake as shown. (Note: each batter board is composed of two sharpened stakes and one horizontal brace, and can be made from scrap 1x4s or 2x4s cut to about 24-inch lengths.) Rather than driving stakes and attaching braces, it's more efficient to assemble each batter board before driving each approximately level with the other.

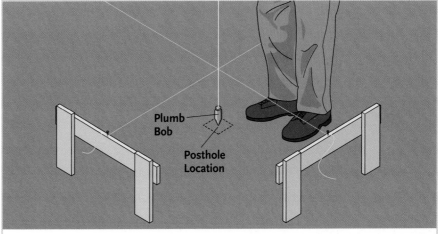

3 **Mark posthole locations.** Use a plumb bob to transfer string line intersections to the posthole locations on the ground.

2 **String the Lines.** Stretch a level string line directly over the first two stakes, and tie it to opposing batter boards, as shown.

To establish the first square corner, use the 3-4-5 rule. Measure from Point A on the first corner stake along the line 3 feet and mark Point B on that string. Next, run a second line perpendicular to the first by stretching the second line over Point A and marking Point C directly on the second string 4 feet from Point A. Then adjust line AC at the far batter board

until distance BC becomes exactly 5 feet. With measurements of 3-4-5 on the sides of the imaginary triangle, angle BAC is now square—your first square corner.

3 **Mark Posthole Locations.** Moving to the second corner stake, install its second batter board, and create the second square corner as you did the first one. In this way, proceed around to all corners. Use a plumb bob, as shown, to transfer line intersections to the ground. Then drive small stakes to mark the intended holes.

4 Check for Square. In the event the final string line doesn't align directly over the first driven stake, your earlier string lines may not be positioned accurately enough. In that case, return to the first stake, the second, and so on, double-checking the 3-4-5 rule at each stake and correcting line positions accordingly. In your confirming check, the distances between opposite diagonal corners of the Central Tower layout (points A1–C3 and A3–C1) should be equal. Always check for level after adjusting string lines.

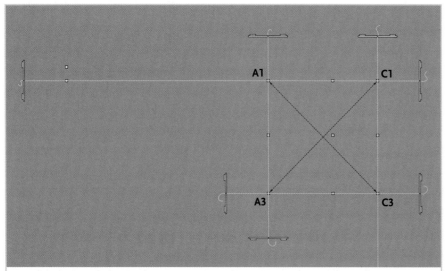

4 Check for Square. When the layout is square, the diagonal distances A1–C3 and A3–C1 will be equal.

SETTING POSTS

The posts should be centered in the holes. Postholes must be dug below frost line, which is the depth to which the ground in your locality will freeze during a cold winter. This requirement helps ensure that no ice forms below the posts, heaving them upward and thereby stressing joints in your structure or even throwing the structure out of alignment. Local building authorities can tell you how deep to dig and, in fact, may insist on inspecting the depth of your holes before allowing you to set the posts in concrete. If you live in a frost-free climate, the posts should be buried at least 36 inches.

As a general rule, postholes should be about three times the diameter of the posts. Thus, for individual 4x4 posts, you should dig 12-inch-diameter holes. For the double post on the free-standing end of the swing, the hole should measure about 12 x 20 inches at the top.

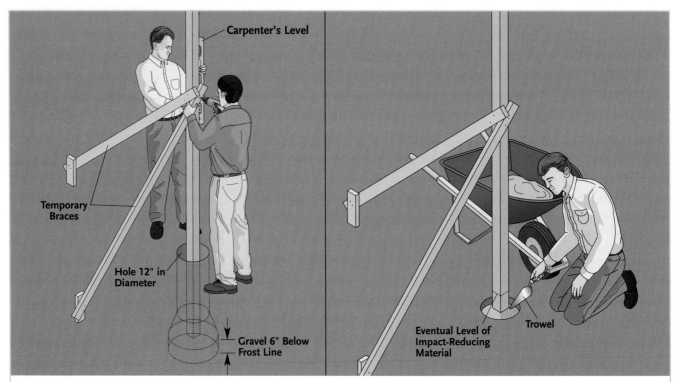

Setting Posts. Center the first post in its hole. When the post is plumb on two adjacent sides, fasten it with bracing. Pour concrete, and use a trowel to slope the wet concrete away from the post, keeping all concrete below ground level.

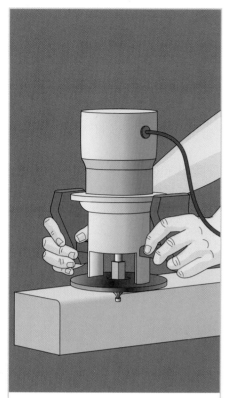

Routing Edges. The most effective tool for rounding edges is the router.

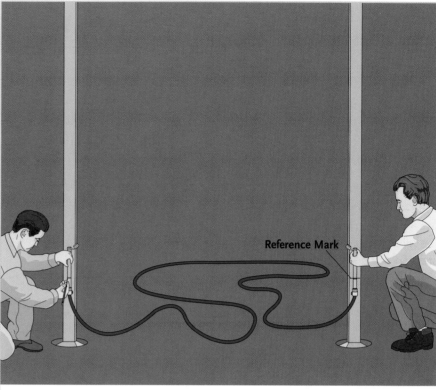

Reference Mark

Using a Water Level. When your carpenter's level won't reach, a simple water level works just as well in transferring your reference mark.

router, and turn it upside down. Drop the bit all the way into the collet, then back it out about ¹⁄₁₆ inch. Tighten the collet nut. Adjust the router for the desired depth of cut. Make a few passes on a piece of scrap wood to ensure that your adjustment is satisfactory. When routing edges, be sure to move the router from left to right (or counterclockwise around a perimeter). Hold the router with both hands, moving it at a comfortable but unforced pace. Always wear eye and ear protection.

USING A WATER LEVEL

A carpenter's level works well on closely spaced posts. But for widely spaced posts, a water level allows you to transfer level marks with deadly accuracy. The device depends on two laws of nature: gravity and atmospheric pressure. Within the hose, water will

seek the same level at each end.

To make your own water level, use ³⁄₈-inch or ⁵⁄₁₆-inch clear vinyl tubing. If you build the kids' playland with all modules, you'll need 26 feet of tubing. Rinse the inside of the tubing with warm water and dish soap to remove any greasy film. Place one end of the tubing in a bucket of clean water. (If you like, you can add a couple drops of oil-free food coloring to make the water more visible.) Hold the other end lower than the bucket, then suck on it until the water starts siphoning in. As soon as water emerges from the lower end, plug that end by placing your thumb over the end of the hose.

Hold both ends of the tubing side-by-side to ensure that the water is level. If it isn't, check the tubing for air bubbles or kinks. Run more water through the tubing to remove air bubbles.

Mark one post with a reference mark at the level you wish to transfer marks to all posts. Place one end of the tubing

against the post, with the water roughly aligned with the reference mark. To keep water from spilling while your helper moves to the post you wish to mark, both of you should place your thumbs over the tube ends. However, to function properly, the tube must be open on each end, and the water must be free of bubbles and able to move freely.

Have a helper position the other end of the tube against the unmarked post. After allowing the shifting water to come to a standstill, the helper should slowly move the tube up or down until the water level at your first reference mark aligns with your original mark. When it does, the helper's water level will be at the correct height. Have the helper mark the second post at that water level.

For best accuracy, continue using your first reference post to repeat the process on as many other posts as your tube will reach.

5 finishing and maintenance

The finish coating you choose will affect the appearance of your play structure. But more important, the finish can affect long-term durability and usability. That is, exterior wood must contend with temperature and moisture changes, the sun's ultraviolet rays, fungi, human use and abuse, and insects. This chapter discusses the variety of exterior finishing products and suggests their advantages and disadvantages.

For outdoor finishes, the principal options are sealers, stains, and paints. The first two are good choices for these projects, but it doesn't make sense to paint unless you are prepared to touch up and repaint regularly. Even a top-notch paint job won't survive the assaults of rambunctious kids.

DURABILITY

If you plan to dismantle the play structure within five years or so, the following strategy lets you avoid finish coatings almost entirely. First, use pressure-treated lumber for posts, beams, joists, and any other members that will be near or will be in contact with the ground. If you choose a premium line of pressure-treated wood, coated with water repellent at the factory, you won't need to apply additional moisture protection for a couple of years. For decking, guardrails, and other parts, you can use the same pressure-treated lumber or choose redwood or cedar heartwood. Left untreated, redwood and cedar will turn gray, but they won't rot or decay for many years.

Many people mistakenly believe that pressure-treated wood does not need to be finished. Although the chemicals used in normal pressure treating are intended to prevent rot and insect damage, they offer no protection against moisture and ultraviolet rays. Also, pressure-treated wood is prone to splitting, regardless of the finish. You can minimize deterioration by applying a stain or a water repellent with ultraviolet (UV) blockers.

If you use untreated wood for the decking and guardrails from a species that isn't rot resistant—such as pine, fir, or hemlock—apply a water-repellent finish that contains preservatives that prevent rot.

SEALERS

Sold as "water repellents," sealers are usually clear or lightly pigmented coatings intended to protect the wood from excessive water absorption. Wood sealers contain a moisture inhibitor, usually paraffin wax, and are commonly sold as deck finishes. You can choose a plain sealer or a sealer with additives that help protect the wood from fungi, mildew, insects, and ultraviolet rays. A sealer that contains UV blockers will maintain the natural wood color for a year or so, while a plain sealer will permit the wood to gray over time. A pigmented sealer will give the wood a moderate tint, without drastically altering its color.

Sealers from different manufacturers may contain different amounts of moisture inhibitor. A high concentration is around 3 percent and is the best choice if you plan to apply only one coat. A sealer with a lower concentration should be regarded as pretreatment, needing another coating.

STAINS

Stains have more pigmentation than sealers. Color options include semitransparent and solid, both available in water-based and oil-based (or alkyd) formulations.

Semitransparent stains are moderately pigmented, adding color while allowing the wood grain to show clearly.

Oil-based semitransparent stains are good choices for pressure-treated wood because they hide the greenish tint. For best results on pressure-treated wood, choose an oil-based stain that mimics red cedar or redwood.

Solid-color stains are essentially thinned paints. They color the whole board, penetrating crevices and defects, sometimes accentuating the grain. But because they form a thin film over the wood, solid-color stains pose the same maintenance problems as paint.

PAINTS

A dash of color can add a playful look to a play structure. But because a play structure takes a lot of abuse, paint can wear away quickly. Not only does deteriorated paint look unattractive, it allows water to seep into the wood and damage it. If you decide to add some paint, consider limiting it to areas that won't receive much abuse. The most durable exterior finish is usually top-quality acrylic latex paint over an alkyd primer.

FINISHING OPTIONS

Use a cedar toner, also called a transparent stain, to simulate the look of more expensive decking.

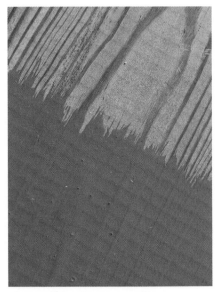

If it's solid color you're after, your best option is an opaque stain.

● SEALERS

When water beads on the wood surface, the water-repellent sealer is doing its job. When water soaks into the wood, it's time to apply more sealer.

PREPARING THE SURFACE

With any finish, the results look better and last longer if you first prepare the surface. If the wood is wet or dirty, the finish won't adhere well and you will need to refinish it sooner.

First, ensure that the wood is reasonably smooth. Wood that hasn't been pressure treated can be given a quick sanding by hand or with a power sander. Sanding allows better penetration of the finish. Because sawdust from pressure-treated wood contains toxic chemicals, sand only enough to remove serious nicks and sharp edges. Wear a dust mask and try to sweep up as much of the chemically treated sawdust as possible for disposal.

If the wood has started to age or if you're just overdue for a refinish job, a deck-cleaning solution can restore the natural color. Most home centers carry the cleaning solution.

Before applying the finish, spray-

A penetrating oil with UV protection, such as this one, will keep its natural wood color—at least for a while.

Semitransparent stains are available in a variety of hues, including the moss green shown here.

Clear sealers, often combined with preservatives, protect wood from moisture penetration.

rinse the entire structure with water to remove sawdust and debris. Use a garden hose with a nozzle that produces a good stream. Then let the wood dry for a day or two.

WHEN TO APPLY THE FINISH

Always follow the manufacturer's instructions on when and how to apply a finish. As a general rule, try to put some finish on the wood as soon as possible; the sun's ultraviolet rays can start adversely affecting the wood almost immediately. If the wood was kiln-dried (KD) or, in the case of treated lumber, kiln-dried after treatment (KDAT) and has been kept dry, you can finish it right away. If the wood is wet, give it a few weeks to dry.

In most cases, water repellent should be applied annually. You can determine if the water repellent needs renewing by splashing water on vertical surfaces. If water beads on the surface instead of penetrating, the repellent is still doing its job. But if the water soaks in, it's time to apply more water repellent.

APPLYING THE FINISH

A brush ensures better penetration than either a roller or a multipurpose sprayer, because it lets you work the finish into the wood. Besides, surfaces on the play structure are relatively small, making a brush about as quick as a roller and less wasteful than a sprayer, which tends to cause overspray. If you do use a sprayer or roller, follow with a brush where possible to work the finish in.

Be sure to read the manufacturer's instructions carefully. For example, some finishes should be recoated before the previous coat dries.

GENERAL MAINTENANCE

Clean the impact-reducing material of debris regularly, the frequency depending on season and use. Sand and gravel need to be raked regularly. Mulch and wood chips should be renewed or replaced when they have begun to decompose or have lost resiliency.

To ensure long life and maximum safety of the Kids' Playland itself, inspect it at least monthly. Replace any metal parts that are especially rusty or otherwise damaged. Check all nuts, tightening as necessary. Inspect ropes and chains for evidence of aging and abuse. Also, remove splinters on all wood surfaces, and sand or remove sharp edges. Touch up nicks in the wood with spare finish.

RENOVATING

If the kids have begun showing less interest in the Kids' Playland, perhaps it is time to do a little renovating. You might consider replacing the Swings with a tire swing, installing a tube slide instead of the straight slide, or adding some other component. Remember, the projects in this book are designed to allow your play structure to grow and mature right along with your children.

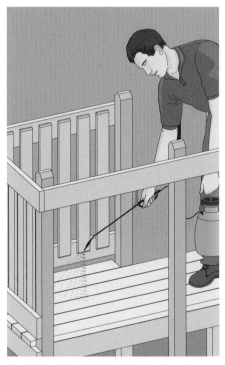

Applying the Finish. Although a pump sprayer is a quick means of applying the finish, you'll get better results if you go over the surface again, brushing the finish in.

Before applying finish, "soften" any sharp edges and corners that you missed prior to construction. The belt sander shown serves well for the purpose but won't reach into corners. For that, use a sanding block and sandpaper.

SAFETY CHECKS

In your regular maintenance inspections, check all nuts and tighten them as necessary. Remember to check the out-of-sight locknuts atop the swing beam. Shown left, the locknut's white bushing helps prevent the nut's working loose under stress.

GENERAL MAINTENANCE

Reapply wood finish as needed.

Check all nuts for tightness.

Inspect for protruding screw or nail heads.

Round-over sharp edges and corners, if you missed any before.

Rake and renew impact-reducing material.

Make maintenance and repair a regular part of your schedule.

PART TWO

In some respects, the entire Kids' Playland—with Central Tower, Swing Beam, and Monkey Bar—is a challenging project in the book. Yet, because it is modular, you can reduce the work by building one module, such as the Central Tower, and adding others later. For structural stability, the posts for all modules should be set in concrete fairly deep in the ground, and the posts need to be positioned precisely. Beyond that, construction is pretty straightforward.

Even so, construction will go easier if you have a helper or two at those moments when you need to position the longer wood members.

KIDS' PLAYLAND

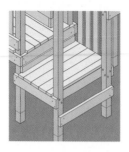

6 kids' playland and its central tower

The Kids' Playland is a multifunction, modular structure that can be adapted to please children of all ages. It provides the basic activities of any successful playground—swinging, sliding, climbing, relaxing, and socializing. All this is in a layout that maximizes safety while using space efficiently.

The optional configuration shown on page 75 can serve children of different ages and energy levels. The floor of the upper level of the Central Tower is 5 feet high—a good compromise height for younger and older children. Although a 5-foot-tall slide may be a bit high for toddlers, it will seem just right to kids over four years old. If you are more interested in satisfying preschoolers, the solution is simple—build at 4 feet and buy a slide designed for that height.

DELUXE CENTRAL TOWER

The Deluxe Version of the Central Tower offers a series of height levels. The lower level serves as a launching pad for the Monkey Bar. The middle level and the additional step combine to offer a seat and space for relaxing play. The first two levels also provide transitions to the upper level. If you don't want the Monkey Bar, and instead prefer a simple ladder for access to the slide, you can opt for the Basic Version of the Central Tower shown on page 89. One virtue of a modular approach to the Playland is that you can later expand the Basic Tower to the Deluxe, shown here.

Our Monkey Bar slopes away from the Central Tower. This allows taller children to use mainly one end and shorter children, the other end. But if you prefer a Monkey Bar that is parallel with the ground, simply install longer posts at the outer end, or reduce the height of the bar where it joins the Tower.

The Swing Beam offers a full 10 feet of clearance between posts. This is plenty of room for two conventional swings, for a single tire swing, or for a set of rings and a trapeze bar. However, if you are pressed for space or simply

kids' playland site layout

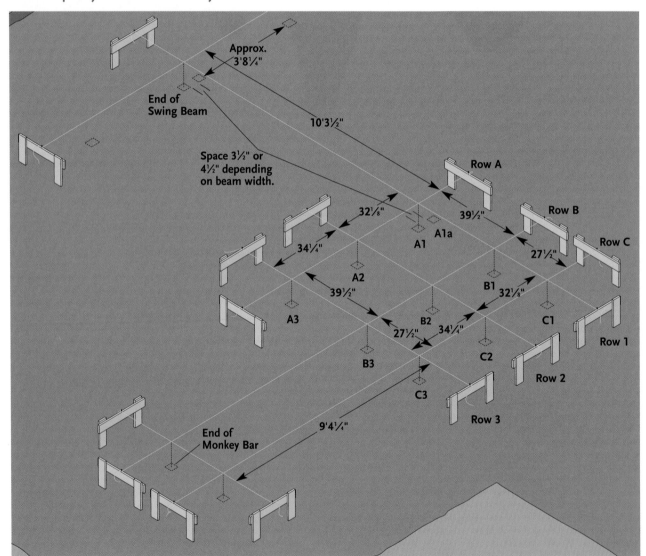

Mark postholes with properly spaced string lines. The Deluxe Version of the Central Tower employs the nine post locations shown clustered in rows 1,2, and 3, plus post A1(a) if you add the Swing Beam. The Basic Version of the Central Tower, shown on page 89, employs just the six post locations shown in rows 1 and 2. (See page 92 for more on the Swing Frame Layout.)

kids' playland with deluxe central tower

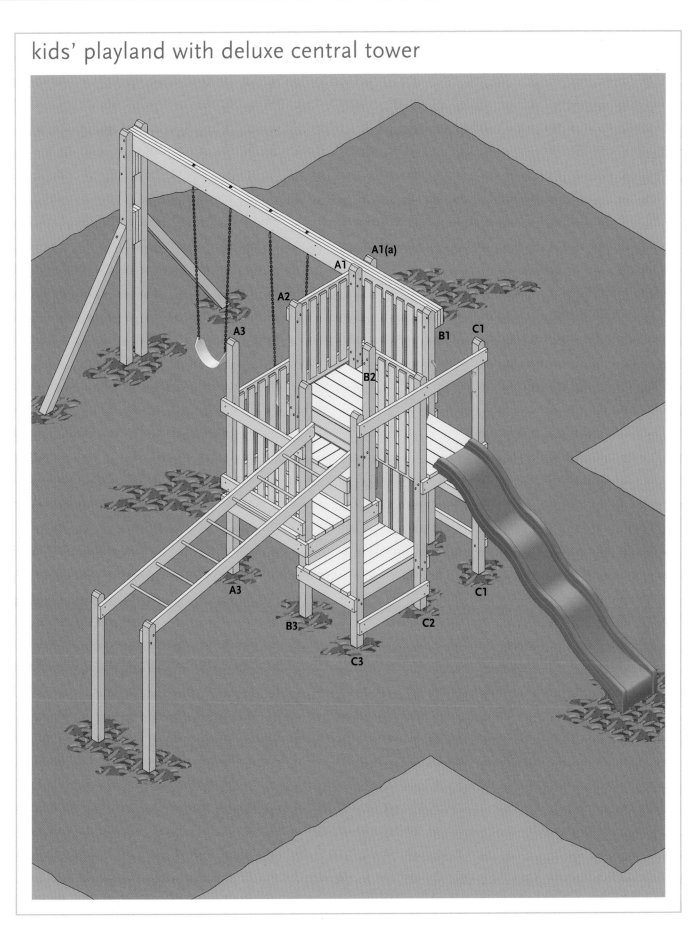

prefer a single conventional swing, you could shorten the beam span to 6½ feet.

Regardless of the configuration, allow sufficient area for the Safety Zone, which should be filled with impact-reducing material, such as wood chips, pea gravel, wood mulch, or sand. You need to decide on impact-reducing material and the configuration of the Safety Zone before you start construction. (See "Layout and Footprint Options" on page 16. There, overhead drawings will help you visualize the safety-zone requirements for optional Playland configurations. For comparisons of impact-reducing materials, including recommended minimum depths, see page 40. Excavate to at least that rec-

ommended minimum before beginning construction.)

Chapter 1 also contains thorough explanations on other safety features incorporated into the design of the various Playland components. As you proceed with construction, refer regularly to Chapter 4 for construction techniques mentioned, in passing, in this chapter and in those that follow.

The full Kids' Playland is constructed in three phases: Central Tower, Swing Frame, and Monkey Bar. The Central Tower is presented in this chapter, and the other components have chapters unto themselves. Although you can build the entire Kids' Playland at once, you can instead build one component at a time, as your time, budget, and en-

ergy allow. If you feel you'll eventually build all components, start with the Central Tower; then add the Swing Frame and the Monkey Bar.

The drawing on page 74 shows dimensions and string-line locations for laying out the full Playland.

Chapters 7 and 8 also explain how you can construct components as stand-alones. Because numerous options are offered in each chapter, review the entire book before finalizing your plans. Chapters 9 through 13 explain, in turn, how to build a Playhouse, sandboxes, two balance beams, a Picnic Table, and a Teeter-Totter. Although these projects are not part of the Kids' Playland, they make great additions to a play yard.

KIDS' PLAYLAND WITH SAFETY ZONES

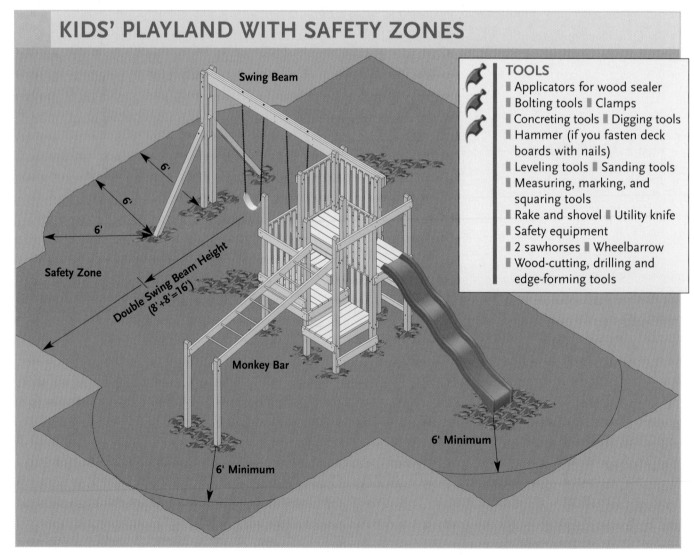

Swing Beam

6'

6'

6'

Safety Zone

Double Swing Beam Height (8' +8' =16')

Monkey Bar

6' Minimum

6' Minimum

TOOLS
- Applicators for wood sealer
- Bolting tools ▮ Clamps
- Concreting tools ▮ Digging tools
- Hammer (if you fasten deck boards with nails)
- Leveling tools ▮ Sanding tools
- Measuring, marking, and squaring tools
- Rake and shovel ▮ Utility knife
- Safety equipment
- 2 sawhorses ▮ Wheelbarrow
- Wood-cutting, drilling and edge-forming tools

THE CENTRAL TOWER

The Central Tower serves various play components, depending on the specific layout option you choose for the Kids' Playland. In the Deluxe Version of the Central Tower shown on previous pages, the upper level provides structural support for one end of the Swing Beam, as well as a platform for entering the slide. Again, if you'd prefer a simpler tower, you could build only the upper level by following instructions for the Basic Version shown on page 89.

Advantages of the Deluxe Version: It has twice the platform surface of the Basic Version. Also, the Deluxe has three levels. The lowest level platform serves the Monkey Bar. The middle level and the step can serve as platforms for sitting, eating, playing card games, or simply daydreaming. The changes in elevation also enhance the Tower's design balance and visual interest.

Preparing the Lumber

It is easier to do the bulk of sanding and smoothing of lumber before construction begins. Round-over the edges of the posts and the top edge of the top rails using a router equipped with a round-over bit. Then smooth all exposed surfaces using a power sander, removing any lumbermill stamps as you go. In addition to providing a surface that is friendlier to small hands, the sanded wood will better absorb the finish you apply.

lumber, materials, and cutting list

LUMBER AND MATERIALS ORDER

Lumber	Quantity	Size
4x4s	9	13' minimum
2x6s	12	8'
	1	10'
	7	12'
2x4s	2	10'
1x4s	1	6'
	14	8'

HARDWARE AND MORE

	Quantity	Size
Carriage bolts, nuts, and washers	98	$3/8$" x 5"
	2	$3/8$" x $6\frac{1}{2}$"
2x6 joist hangers and nails	8	2
Deck screws	250	3"
	150	2"
Plastic slide	1	10'
Handles, Concrete, Gravel, Finish, Impact-reducing material		

CUTTING LIST

Lumber	Quantity	Size
Posts 4x4	9	13' min.
Joists 2x6	1	21"
	1	$25\frac{5}{8}$"
	1	$30\frac{5}{8}$"
	3	31"
	1	$35\frac{5}{8}$"
	1	$37\frac{1}{8}$"
	5	$37\frac{3}{4}$"
	1	43"
	2	46"
	1	$70\frac{1}{2}$"
Decking 2x6	3	$35\frac{3}{4}$"
	5	$40\frac{3}{4}$"
	6	46"
	5	$73\frac{1}{2}$"
Rails 2x6	1	31"
	2	$35\frac{3}{8}$"
	2	38"
	2	$44\frac{1}{2}$"
	1	$69\frac{7}{8}$"
Stair 2x6	2	9"
	9	12"
	2	33"
	2	36"
Step 2x6	1	$37\frac{3}{4}$"
Steps 2x4	3	31"
Nailing cleats 2x4	6	4–5"
Blocking 2x4	1	$37\frac{3}{4}$"
	1	43"
Balusters 1x4	22	36"
	4	46"
	4	42"

LAYING OUT THE SITE

If you are planning to build the full Kids' Playland, see pages 92-93 for instructions on laying out the site for all components. This chapter addresses laying out the Deluxe Central Tower alone, but simplified layout for the Basic Tower is readily apparent along post rows 1 and 2. See "Setting the Posts," below.

Note that the Site Layout drawing on page 74 labels the rows and posts. Be sure to refer to these labels regularly during construction.

Use batter boards and strings to establish the positions for all nine posts for the Central Tower (ten if you will add the Swing Beam now or later). Space the string lines exactly as shown in the Site Layout. Each intersection of string lines marks the center of a post. Drop a plumb line at each intersection and mark the ground using a small stake, such as a scrap piece of wood. When all posthole locations are marked, remove the strings, and dig nine 12-inch-diameter holes to at least 3 feet deep no matter where you live, and to an additional 6 inches below frost line if you live in a northern state or Canada. Pour 6 inches of gravel into each hole.

SETTING THE POSTS

The normal procedure for setting posts is to carefully brace each post before adding concrete to the hole. But with nine posts in close proximity and the need to space them accurately, you will be better off building a temporary frame that lets you align all posts at once.

1 Mark the Temporary Frame. Make the frame using the 8-foot 1x4s you bought to use as balusters. Since you'll reuse boards in the temporary

frame for balusters later, mark them lightly in pencil now and use a minimal number of screws or nails. The drawing shows how to mark the 1x4s so that they won't need to be cut for use on the temporary frame. To position the nine posts, you'll need 14 total boards, six each with post positions marked 12 inches from the right end, plus two corner braces.

2 Attach the Temporary Frame. With a couple of helpers, you may be able to attach the 1x4s to the posts without needing any diagonal braces into the ground. But even if help is available, we recommend diagonal

bracing for the first post, basing all other posts on the first.

Frame the four outside posts first (A1, A3, C1, and C3). Once they are up, the other posts will be easier to attach. Set post A1 into its hole. Then measure up the post about 12 inches and 72 inches above ground level, marking each location. While helpers or braces hold posts A1 and A3 upright, attach the 1x4 for Row A at 12 inches. Drive a 2-inch screw or a 6d duplex nail through the board into post A1; then use a level to position the board on post A3. Move up to the 72-inch mark on post A1 and repeat the process.

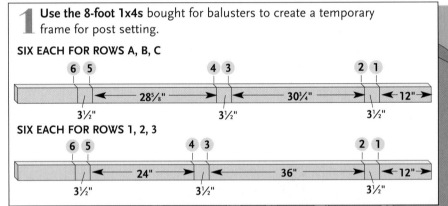

1 **Use the 8-foot 1x4s** bought for balusters to create a temporary frame for post setting.

SIX EACH FOR ROWS A, B, C

⑥ ⑤   ④ ③   ② ①
                28⅝"   30¾"   12"
3½"   3½"   3½"

SIX EACH FOR ROWS 1, 2, 3

⑥ ⑤   ④ ③   ② ①
                24"   36"   12"
3½"   3½"   3½"

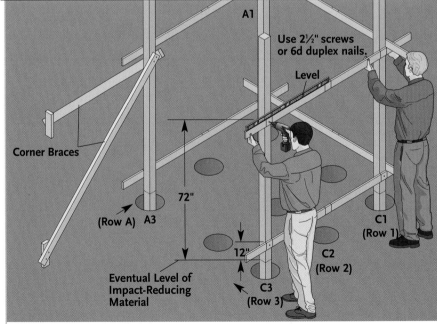

A1

Use 2½" screws or 6d duplex nails.

Level

Corner Braces

72"

(Row A) A3

12"

Eventual Level of Impact-Reducing Material

C1 (Row 1)

C2 (Row 2)

C3 (Row 3)

2 **After bracing the first post** (here A3) true and plumb, use it as reference and support in attaching temporary braces to the other three corners. Align the posts with the reference marks on the 1x4s.

Brace or have a helper hold Row A upright while you set post C1 in its hole. Rest a 1x4 for Row 1 on top of one of the boards already attached to post A1; then use a level to position the board on post C1. Fasten the board to the two posts.

Repeat this process on Row C, placing post C3 in its hole. But place the boards directly beneath the overhanging boards on post C1. The two boards you will install on Row 3, then, should rest on top of the overhanging boards you've already installed.

With the four corners framed, ensure that all posts are plumb and that the structure is square. The structure will be square when the diagonal distances between corner posts are equal. Then continue adding posts and boards. When the frame is complete,

check again for plumb and square.

Add concrete to each hole to 3 inches below ground level, sloping the concrete away from the posts, as shown on page 54. Let the concrete cure undisturbed overnight. Then remove the lower boards of the temporary frame so that they won't be damaged during subsequent construction. Leave the upper boards in place for now because they add stability to the posts. You can remove those boards one at a time when they would otherwise interfere with construction.

■ **Marking the Reference Line.** The best way to ensure that your decks are level is to establish a reference mark on one post and then transfer this mark to all posts supporting that deck. If you were to proceed instead from post to post, measuring from the ground up,

it is unlikely that the reference lines would be level.

Using a tape measure (above the eventual level of impact-reducing material), make a mark on one post at 60 inches, which is the finished deck height of the upper level. Then use a 4-foot carpenter's level to transfer this mark to each of the posts. If you don't have a 4-foot level, you can rest a 2-footer on a longer, straight board, or use a water level, as shown on page 63.

Use a combination square to extend the reference point around all four sides of each post. Mark this line 60" so that it remains distinguishable from layout lines to come. This is an important detail because in the following instructions, the dimensions for much of the construction will be given from this reference point.

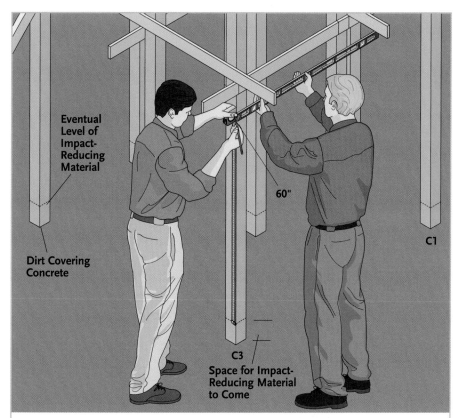

Eventual Level of Impact-Reducing Material

Dirt Covering Concrete

60"

C1

C3

Space for Impact-Reducing Material to Come

Marking the Reference Line. With the posts in concrete, establish level for each deck based on one reference mark, transferring that reference by means of a level, as shown, or by means of a water level. Note the allowance for the depth of impact-reducing material yet to come. See page 40 for recommended depths.

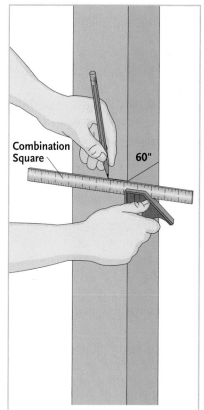

Combination Square

60"

Marking the Post. After transferring the reference line by means of a level, use a square to extend the reference lines around all of the posts.

FRAMING THE TOWER

The three levels on the Central Tower are framed independently. Each level has four rim joists that are bolted to posts. A total of four additional joists are needed, which are attached to the rim joists using joist hangers.

Because rim joists meet at right angles on most posts, with bolts running through posts at right angles, position bolts so they don't run into each other. The best approach is to stagger the bolts in a systematic manner, as described and illustrated below.

Note: Throughout this book, exact dimensions are given for each joist. These dimensions assume that each post is located exactly as shown in the layout and is perfectly plumb, and that the entire structure is perfectly square. Chances are, however, that your dimensions will vary somewhat, so be sure to measure each joist spacing before cutting.

The simplest and most prudent technique for attaching rim joists is to measure and cut each joist, one at a time. Then measure and mark the bolt-hole layout, and fasten the joist to the post temporarily using screws driven through the bolt-hole markings. To drill the bolt holes, remove one screw and drill a bolt hole in its place. Insert a bolt and hand tighten it; then remove the other screw and repeat the process. When you have installed all bolts for each level, go back and tighten the nuts using a socket wrench.

■ **Staggering Bolt Holes.** The rim joists must be bolted securely to the posts. If bolted correctly, your frame will be strong. But a careless approach to drilling bolt holes can weaken the posts and jeopardize the structural integrity of the entire tower.

There are several essentials: use the proper-size bolt. In this project, ⅜-inch bolts are specified for every

● RECESSING HARDWARE

Avoid allowing any hardware to protrude in a way that a child might bump it or snag clothing on it. This requires that most of the washers and nuts be installed in recess holes drilled into the posts. Begin by temporarily fastening a 2x6 to its posts. Then follow the steps below.

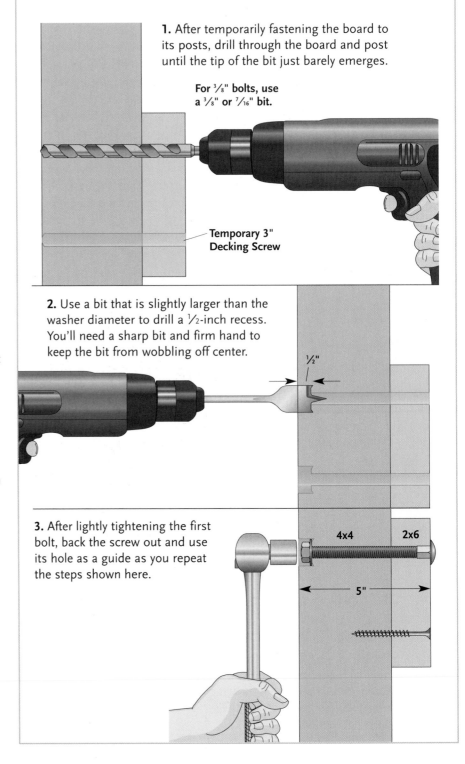

1. After temporarily fastening the board to its posts, drill through the board and post until the tip of the bit just barely emerges.

For ⅜" bolts, use a ⅜" or ⁷⁄₁₆" bit.

Temporary 3" Decking Screw

2. Use a bit that is slightly larger than the washer diameter to drill a ½-inch recess. You'll need a sharp bit and firm hand to keep the bit from wobbling off center.

½"

3. After lightly tightening the first bolt, back the screw out and use its hole as a guide as you repeat the steps shown here.

4x4   2x6

5"

application except the Swing Frame.

Second, as shown on the next page, bolts on the same side of a post should be staggered vertically, to minimize splitting of the post. Otherwise, bolts or other fasteners aligned vertically along the same grain lines in wood greatly increase the likelihood of splitting the wood.

Third, bolts passing through adjacent sides of a post must be staggered so they allow sufficient room for clearance. Bolt holes that cross too close to each other can interfere with bolt placement and weaken the post. The inset drawing on page 82 shows a safe approach for staggering bolt holes in each post. Measure and mark the layout on each rim joist before drilling any holes.

■ **Frame the Lower Level.** The lower frame attaches to posts B2, B3, C2, and C3. On each post, measure down from the 60-inch reference point exactly 37½ inches. (See page 82.) Mark this location; then align the tops of each joist with this line. Cut two 31-inch and two 37¾-inch rim joists and attach them to the posts as shown. Use ⅜ x 5-inch carriage bolts at each connection. Note that the bolts in accompanying drawings show on which sides the bolts should be inserted; the object is to try to drill recesses in the thick 4x4 posts, rather than into the joists.

After bolting the rim joists to the posts, cut and install the center joist using 2x6 joist hangers. Center this joist between the two longer rim joists.

■ **Frame the Middle Level.** The middle level attaches to posts A2, A3, B2, and B3. On each post, measure down from the 60-inch reference point exactly 25½ inches. Mark this location, and then align the tops of each joist with this line. Cut two 46-inch and two 37¾-inch rim joists and attach them to the posts as shown. Use ⅜ x 5-inch carriage bolts at each connection.

After bolting the rim joists to the

posts, cut and install the center joist using 2x6 joist hangers. Center this between the two longer rim joists.

■ **Frame the Upper Level.** The upper level attaches to posts A1, A2, B1, B2, C1, and C2. Measure down from the 60-inch reference point exactly 1½ inches to determine the alignment for the tops of each joist. Again, based on your own post-to-post distances, cut

rim joists of about 70½ inches, 43 inches, 37⅛ inches, 35⅝ inches, and 31 inches. Attach the joists to the posts as shown. Use ⅜ x 5-inch carriage bolts on all connections except at post B1, where you will need a longer 6½-inch bolt. Remember to drill the recess into the joist on the inside of the post. Cut inside joists of 30⅝ and 25⅝ inches; installing 2x6 joist hangers.

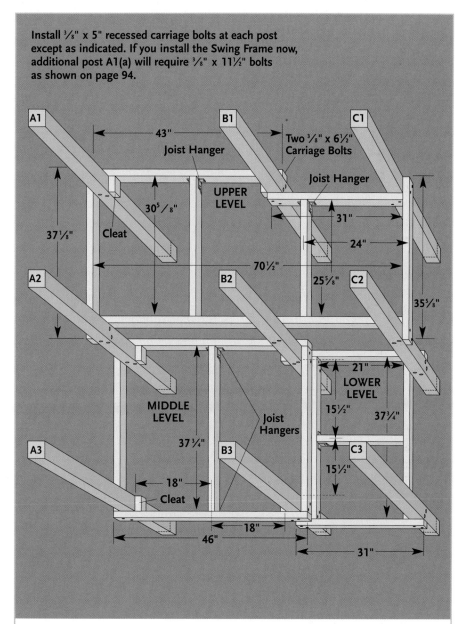

Install ⅜" x 5" recessed carriage bolts at each post except as indicated. If you install the Swing Frame now, additional post A1(a) will require ⅜" x 11½" bolts as shown on page 94.

Frame Dimensions for Each Level. All dimensions shown are based on perfect placements of all posts. Thus, you should consider the dimensions approximate, adjusting them as needed to match your exact post-to-post distances. (See page 82 for recessed fastener information.)

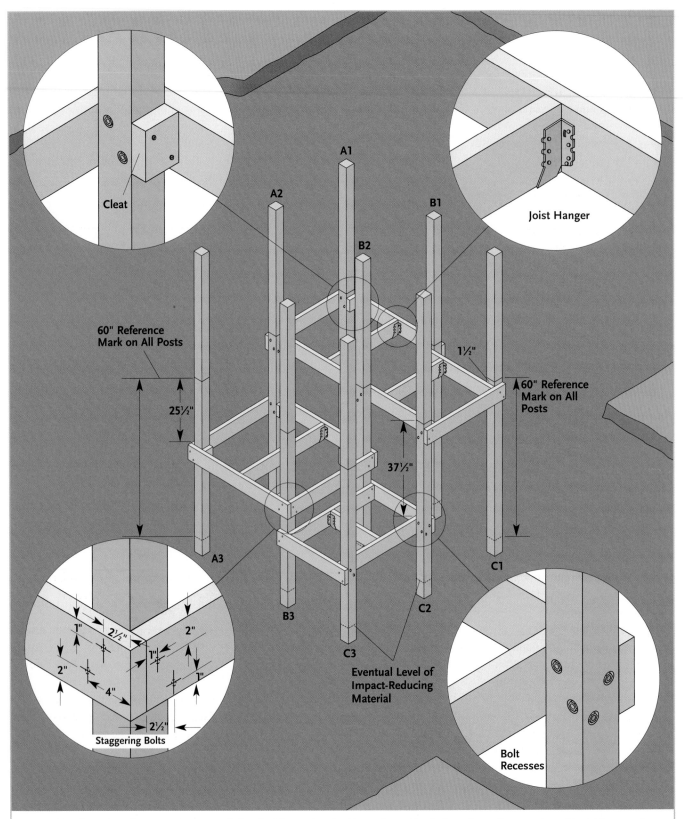

Cleat

A1

A2

B2

B1

Joist Hanger

60" Reference Mark on All Posts

1½"

60" Reference Mark on All Posts

25½"

37½"

A3

C1

B3

C2

2½"

1"

2"

1"

2"

1"

2"

4"

1"

2½"

Staggering Bolts

C3

Eventual Level of Impact-Reducing Material

Bolt Recesses

Framing the Central Tower. Frame each level independently. Note distances below the reference line. Begin by attaching rim joists to posts temporarily using screws. Then remove screws one at a time, replacing each with a bolt. Stagger bolts so they won't hit one another or weaken joints, and recess nuts on the post side. Cleats will support deck boards that will have no joists to rest on.

INSTALLING THE DECKING

The framing allows for decking boards on the middle level to be installed perpendicular to those on the lower level. The decking boards on the middle and upper levels are installed parallel with each other, but the treads on the stair between the levels (to be built later) will run perpendicular to the decking. These contrasting decking patterns add design interest and also promote safety by drawing attention to the changes in levels. For tips on installation, see page 59.

Most of the decking boards will be full-width 2x6s. A few of the 2x6s will need to be ripped narrower to allow a good fit. You could instead insert an occasional 2x4 or 2x8; so, with careful planning, you may not need to rip any decking boards. The illustrations offer specific suggestions for board widths, assuming a 1/8-inch gap between all boards, and between boards and posts. Use these suggestions as a guide to determine the best widths of decking boards for each level on your tower.

■ **Installing Cleats.** Note that the middle level and the upper level require the installation of 2x4 cleats to create fastening surfaces for some decking boards. Cut these cleats from scrap 2x4s; each should be 4 to 5 inches long. Use 3-inch screws to fasten each cleat to its post, but only after you have tightened the nuts beneath them. Once or twice a year you should tighten all of the nuts on the structure. The screw-fastened cleats are easy to remove for this purpose and then reinstall.

Fasten the decking boards to the joists using 3-inch decking screws or 16d nails. Use two fasteners at each junction, spaced about 1 inch from the edge. When fastening a decking board near its ends, drill pilot holes first to prevent splitting.

■ **Install Lower-Level Decking.** Each of the decking boards on the lower

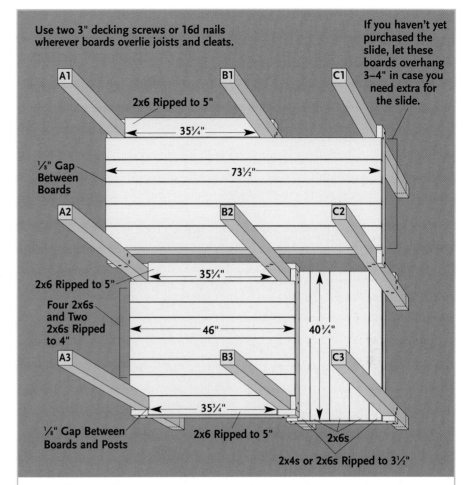

Use two 3" decking screws or 16d nails wherever boards overlie joists and cleats.

If you haven't yet purchased the slide, let these boards overhang 3–4" in case you need extra for the slide.

2x6 Ripped to 5"

35¾"

1/8" Gap Between Boards

73½"

2x6 Ripped to 5"

Four 2x6s and Two 2x6s Ripped to 4"

35¾"

46"

40¾"

1/8" Gap Between Boards and Posts

2x6 Ripped to 5"

2x6s

2x4s or 2x6s Ripped to 3½"

Installing Decking. Attach decking boards flush with the rim joists, equally spaced. Note that the middle and upper levels need nailing cleats for boards that won't rest on joists.

level is 40¾ inches long. Using 2x4s on each end along with three 2x6s allows for a good fit. Use two fasteners wherever boards overlie joists or cleats.

■ **Install Middle-Level Decking.** The two end boards must fit between the posts. Cut each to 35¾ inches to allow gaps. By ripping each board to exactly 5 inches, each will line up with the posts and simplify placement of the rest of the decking. Attach cleats to each post, as shown opposite, before installing the end boards.

The other decking boards are 46 inches long. Two of the boards have been ripped to a width of 4 inches and are installed apart from one another among the full-width 2x6s.

■ **Install Upper-Level Decking.** The short board between posts A1 and B1 must be cut to a length of 35¾ inches. This board should also be ripped to a width of 5 inches. Attach supporting cleats to each post before installing this board.

The other five boards are full-width 2x6s. If you are planning to install a slide, you may need to let these boards overhang the slide's rim joist by several inches to allow the slide to be bolted to the deck. Check the instructions accompanying your commercially made slide before proceeding.

If you don't yet have the slide, install boards that are at least 77 inches long. Later, you can cut them if necessary to accommodate the slide.

INSTALLING MIDDLE- AND UPPER-LEVEL RAILS

The locations for the 2x6 rails are all based on the decking surface. The rails are fastened to the posts in the same manner as the rim joists. Since children will touch top edges of the top rails regularly, the edges should be rounded and smoothed.

Cut the rails to length and then fasten them temporarily to the posts using screws. Next, remove the screws one at a time as you replace them by drilling bolt holes and installing bolts. As with the joists, the washers and nuts should be recessed on the post side of the connection, and the bolts should be offset and staggered, as shown on page 82.

The middle level has two top and two bottom rails, which meet at post A3. The bottom of the bottom rails should be positioned 2 inches above the decking surface, and the top of the top rails should be 42 inches above the surface of the decking.

The rails on the upper level are a bit more complicated to prepare and install. The two bottom rails, which meet at post A1, are also located 2 inches above the decking surface. However, the tops of the three top rails are at $41\frac{1}{2}$ inches; this allows the top rail between posts A1 and A2 to align with the bottom edge of the Swing Beam, when it has been installed.

Note: If you do not intend to install the Swing Beam right away, you will need to install a $44\frac{1}{2}$-inch top rail between posts A1 and B1.

The rail between posts C1 and C2 actually continues to post C3. It serves as a handle to help guide children onto the slide while also providing lateral bracing. Note that if you do not intend to install a slide immediately, you will need to install a $35\frac{5}{8}$-inch bottom rail between posts C1 and C2 in addition

to the $69\frac{7}{8}$-inch top rail shown in the illustration below. For safety reasons, the balusters in this bay are installed differently.

Only a top rail is installed between posts C2 and B2. That is because the balusters in this bay will be installed on the back side of the rail, and they will extend and be fastened to the joist beneath the decking. (See "Special Baluster Treatment" and the drawing opposite.)

INSTALLING BALUSTERS

The 1x4 balusters are installed vertically, attached to the inside top and bottom rails. The actual width of a 1x4 ($3\frac{1}{2}$ inches) is the maximum gap recommended by the U.S. Consumer Product Safety Commission. Local code may require less. Other choices for balusters include 1x6s and 2x2s.

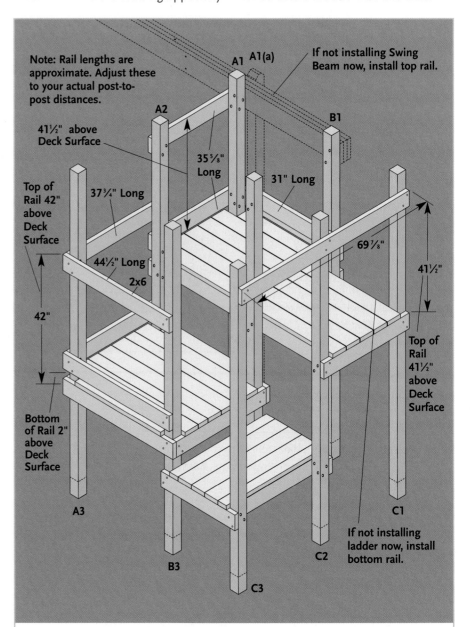

Note: Rail lengths are approximate. Adjust these to your actual post-to-post distances.

A1 A1(a)

If not installing Swing Beam now, install top rail.

A2

$41\frac{1}{2}$" above Deck Surface

$35\frac{5}{8}$" Long

B1

31" Long

Top of Rail 42" above Deck Surface

$37\frac{3}{4}$" Long

$69\frac{7}{8}$"

$44\frac{1}{2}$" Long

2x6

$41\frac{1}{2}$"

42"

Top of Rail $41\frac{1}{2}$" above Deck Surface

Bottom of Rail 2" above Deck Surface

A3

B3

C1

C2

C3

If not installing ladder now, install bottom rail.

Bolt the rails to the posts in the same manner as the rim joists. The top rail on the upper level is positioned to align with the Swing Beam. See the text for rail installation guidance if you do not intend to install the Swing Beam now.

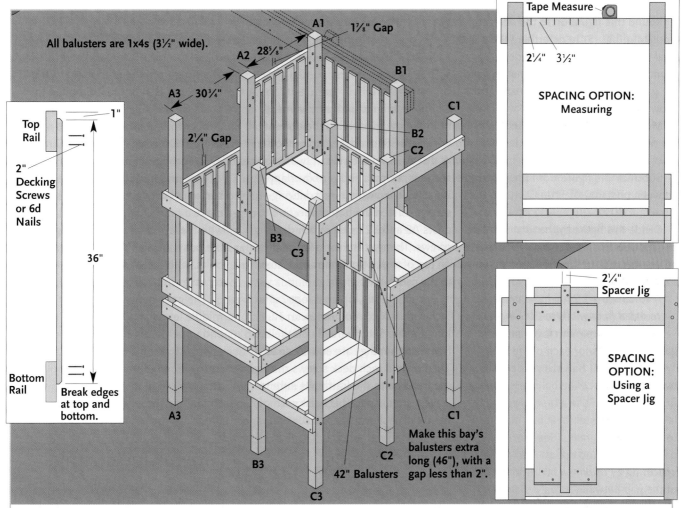

All balusters are 1x4s (3½" wide).

A1 — 1⅞" Gap
A2 — 28⅝"
A3 — 30¾"
2¼" Gap
B1
B2
B3
C1
C2
C3

Top Rail — 1"
2" Decking Screws or 6d Nails
36"
Bottom Rail — Break edges at top and bottom.

Tape Measure
2¼"   3½"
SPACING OPTION: Measuring

2¼" Spacer Jig
SPACING OPTION: Using a Spacer Jig

42" Balusters
Make this bay's balusters extra long (46"), with a gap less than 2".

Installing Balusters. To space balusters evenly, calculate the baluster gap (see text). Break the sharp edges before fastening balusters to the rails. Install balusters above the lower level so that little hands can't reach the upper deck.

● SPECIAL BALUSTER TREATMENT

As a safety measure, the balusters between posts B2 and C2 should be installed a bit differently. To understand the following explanation, consult the drawing above.

If the balusters at the upper level were installed conventionally, there would be a gap between the decking and the bottom rail. This gap would be large enough for a child to slip its fingers through, where they might be stepped on by someone on the upper deck.

To remove this hazard, run the balusters all the way from the top rail to the joist beneath the upper level decking. Also, keep the gap between these balusters less than 2 inches. Using these precautions, you will have made it more difficult for little hands from the lower level to find their way onto the upper deck.

For appearance's sake, try to maintain consistent spacing. The following explains how to calculate the gaps.

■ **Calculating the Baluster Gap.** Calculate baluster spacing for each bay (that is, each section of railing between two posts). First, decide on the approximate gap you want (3½ inches is the maximum allowed by the U.S. Consumer Products Safety Commission). Add this figure to the width of one baluster (3½ inches when using 1x4s):

$$3½ + 3½ = 7$$

Measure the distance between the posts (30¾ inches in the bay between posts A2 and A3), and divide that dimension by the baluster width plus gap amount:

$$30¾ ÷ 7 = 4.4$$

85

FINISHING TOUCHES

You can now proceed to install the Swing Frame and the Monkey Bar, if that is your intention (see upcoming chapters). Before allowing the Central Tower to be used, apply the finish of your choice, and install the impact-reducing material as described in Chapter 4.

The open area beneath the upper level is just about the right size to appeal to young children as a shady spot to sit and relax—and it is. The problem with children playing in this area is that the frame for the upper deck is within easy reach, and protruding nails or screws, the sharp edges of joist hangers, and splintering lumber could all cause injury.

To make this open area safer, there are two options. The first is simply to close it off with diagonal bracing, not shown here. Although your Central Tower shouldn't require any additional bracing (your local building inspector may say otherwise), you can install several 2x4s diagonally between posts. Diagonal, rather than horizontal, installation reduces the likelihood that adventurous souls will use the 2x4s as steps to climb from the outside. To further discourage climbing, attach the diagonal 2x4s to the insides of the posts and joists with nails or decking screws. The most useful locations for this barrier are between posts A1 and A2, A1 and B1, and C1 and C2.

The second option is to allow access to the space beneath the upper level but block access to protruding hardware in the framing above. You don't want to completely cover the framing because that will inhibit water from draining. Instead, staple chicken wire or small-mesh plastic fencing to the undersides of joists.

Tip: Don't forget to round over any sharp edges using a router. Check to be sure all nuts and screws are tight.

● THE SLIDING POLE

A sliding "firefighter's" pole is always a hit with kids. On the Central Tower, a sliding pole is a good choice if you aren't installing a slide. The pole must be installed far enough away from the structure to make the descent safe yet close enough to allow safe access. Make the pole using galvanized steel plumbing pipe and fittings; you should use at least 1-inch (nominal) pipe, which has an outside diameter of about 1½ inches.

Attach the flange to the post with 3-inch lag screws, not simple wood screws, to ensure a secure connection. The pole should be braced at the bottom by burying it at least 24 inches deep. To bury the pole, dig a hole 6 to 8 inches in diameter. With the 10-foot pipe resting on a large, flat rock in the hole, assemble the pipe and fittings as shown. Backfill the hole with dirt, tamping it firmly every 6 inches with a 2x4. To add a dash of color, paint the pole brightly before installation. Be sure to surround the bottom of the pole with extra impact-reducing material.

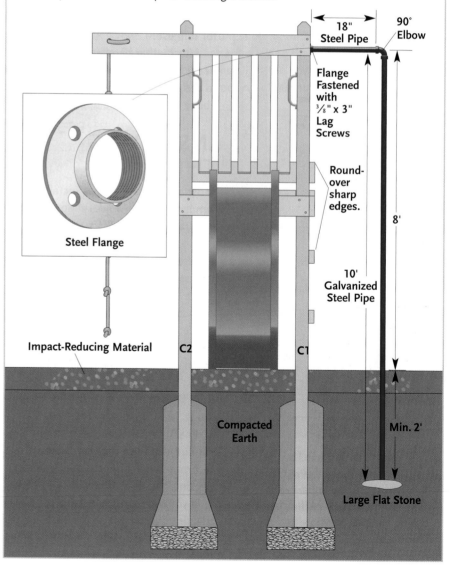

18"
Steel Pipe

90°
Elbow

Flange Fastened with ⅜" x 3" Lag Screws

Round-over sharp edges.

8'

Steel Flange

10' Galvanized Steel Pipe

Impact-Reducing Material

C2

C1

Compacted Earth

Min. 2'

Large Flat Stone

THE BASIC VERSION OF THE CENTRAL TOWER

The accompanying Basic Version of the Central Tower has about half the footprint of the Deluxe Version. Yet with a little planning, the Basic Version can offer a worthy variety of activities.

Referring back to the Playland Site Layout on page 74, you'll note that placement for the six posts needed for the Basic Version is shown along rows 1 and 2. Thus the layout for the Basic Tower allows you to expand it to the Deluxe Tower at a later date, following the layout and instructions in this chapter. In either case, you need to set the posts in concrete and fasten the joists, decking, rails, and balusters in the same way.

The drawing of this Basic Version shows optional accessories. In addition to a climbing rope, climbing nets are available at reasonable cost from manufacturers of playground equipment. Follow manufacturer instructions for installation.

Like the Deluxe Version, the Basic Version of the Central Tower can be built with a deck height of 48 inches, which is better than 60 inches for younger children. A 48-inch deck height is ideal for an 8-foot-long slide.

The Basic Version can include a swing frame large enough for a single swing. If you are building the deck at the lower 48 inches, you might prefer a lower swing-beam height as well. (See Chapter 7 for more on the Swing Frame.)

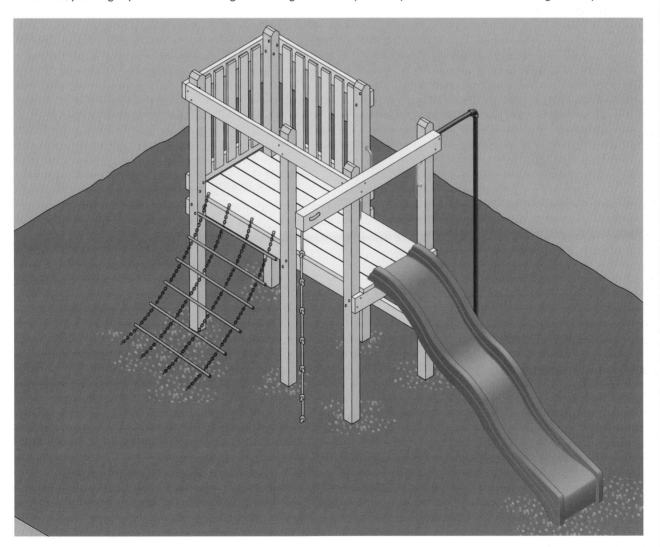

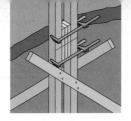

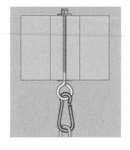

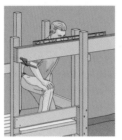

7 swing frame

Swings are almost as vital to a children's playground as tires are to a car. Surely no other project in this book would be used as much by so many children—and adults.

And yet many backyard swing sets sit idle while their intended users head for the swings at school or at the park. There's a good reason for this preference: many backyard swings are small, flimsy structures made of tubular metal and allow only a short swing arc. They are best for very young children who can't propel themselves. Once kids leave the kiddie seat and learn to kick and pump on their own, they crave speed and altitude.

The plans in this chapter show how you can make a Swing Frame that kids won't ignore. Plus the swings shown here are detachable, so the swing set grows with the children.

SWING-FRAME BASICS

The swing beam—the horizontal member that supports the swings—is 8 feet above the impact-reducing material, allowing a substantial and satisfying swing arc. On one end, the beam is fastened to three posts on the Central Tower; on the other end, it is fastened to a double post with an A-frame. With this arrangement, even an aggressive swinger won't affect the stability of the structure.

For safety's sake, the beam is oversized to support kids and parents alike. And the distance between posts allows swings to be spaced far enough apart to ensure that two simultaneous swingers won't collide.

Although called a Swing Frame, this project can be used for a number of optional swinging and gymnastic accessories. The full-length Swing Frame is long enough to allow for the safe use of a tire swing. But because a tire swing moves in all directions, it should be the only accessory suspended from the beam; all others should be removed. Also, the bottom of the tire should be at least 24 inches above ground, thereby minimizing the chance for the user to bump a post.

As alternatives, rings, trapeze bars, and climbing ropes can be attached to the Swing Frame. But again, any accessory that allows swinging from side to side should be the only accessory attached at any one time. Changing accessories can be a breeze if you first attach a series of eyebolts on the beam, and use quick-release fasteners.

You'll find additional instructions if you need or prefer a Swing Frame suitable for only a single swing, or if you decide to build the Swing Frame as a stand-alone unit. Regardless of the design you choose, bear in mind that swings are perhaps the most dangerous component on any playground. The person using the swing can be in-

jured from an accidental fall as well as from intended "jumps" from the swing while it is moving. But the most serious swing accidents occur to children who run into the path of a moving swing, colliding either with the person using the swing or with the seat.

Take these safety precautions:

■ Extend the impact-reducing material at least double the swing height in front and in back, and 6 feet outside each post.

■ Locate the swing away from any pathways that children are likely to use to reach the other parts of the Kids' Playland. This can be accomplished by placing the swing adjacent to bushes or a fence, or by adding a simple rope fence around the perimeter.

■ Use safe, flexible seats on the swings that have no protruding hardware and no hard edges. (For a more complete discussion of safety, see Chapter 1, page 8.)

SITE LAYOUT

If you are building the Swing Frame when you build the Central Tower, you can dig all postholes then; this is especially advised if you rent a power auger. The illustrations show the string-line layouts, based on whether the Central Tower is in place. Note that dimensions differ on the two illustrations, indicating different alignments with post A—either splitting the middle or locating the edge of the post.

lumber and materials order

LUMBER

Lumber	Quantity	Size
4x4s	3	13' minimum
	2	10'
2x8s	3	16'

HARDWARE AND MORE

Materials	Quantity	Size
Fasteners		
Carriage bolts, nuts, and washers	6	$\frac{3}{8}$" x 5"
	2	$\frac{3}{8}$" x 8"
	4	$\frac{1}{2}$" x 8"
	11	$\frac{1}{2}$" x 12"
Carriage bolt or threaded rod	1	$\frac{1}{2}$" x 16"
Eyebolts, locking nuts, washers	4	$\frac{3}{8}$" x 8"
S-hooks	8	$\frac{3}{8}$" x 2$\frac{1}{2}$"
Spring-loaded clips	4	$\frac{3}{8}$" x 3$\frac{1}{2}$"
Chain		
Swing seats		
Concrete		
Gravel		
Impact-reducing material		
Finish		

SWING-FRAME BASICS

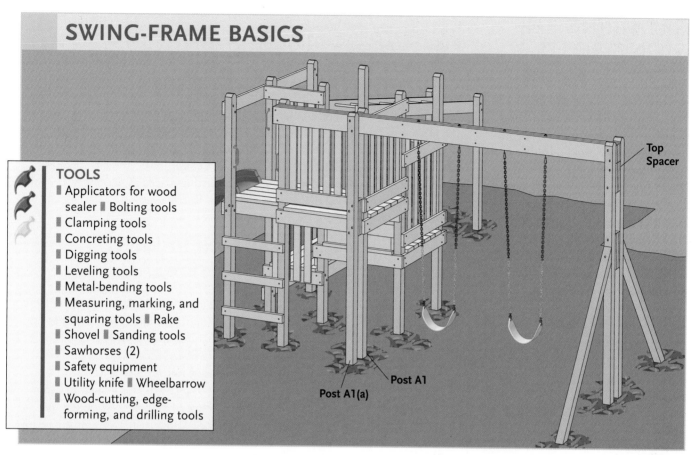

TOOLS

- Applicators for wood sealer ▌Bolting tools
- Clamping tools
- Concreting tools
- Digging tools
- Leveling tools
- Metal-bending tools
- Measuring, marking, and squaring tools ▌Rake
- Shovel ▌Sanding tools
- Sawhorses (2)
- Safety equipment
- Utility knife ▌Wheelbarrow
- Wood-cutting, edge-forming, and drilling tools

Top Spacer

Post A1

Post A1(a)

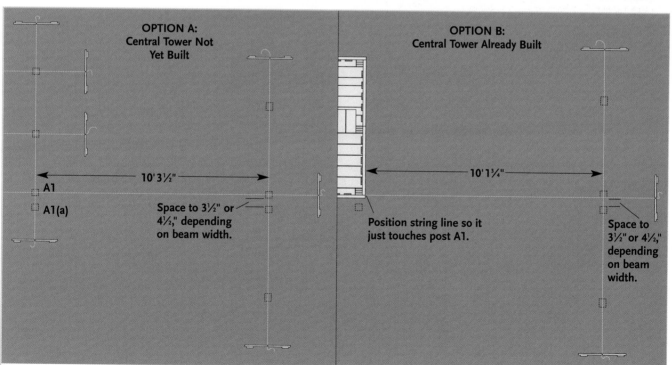

OPTION A:
Central Tower Not Yet Built

10' 3½"

A1

A1(a)

Space to 3½" or 4½," depending on beam width.

OPTION B:
Central Tower Already Built

10' 1¾"

Position string line so it just touches post A1.

Space to 3½" or 4½," depending on beam width.

Site Layout. If you will dig postholes for the Swing Frame at the time you dig holes for the Central Tower, use the layout shown in Option A. However, if you dig postholes after constructing the Central Tower, use Option B. If you build the Central Tower only and anticipate adding the Swing Frame later, allow sufficient room for an eventual post A1(a) and its concrete footing.

PREPARING THE SWING POSTS

Because the outer posthole and the posthole for posts A1 and A1(a) will receive two spaced 4x4 posts, they must be larger than holes for single posts. The depth should be the same, at least 3 feet, plus at least 6 inches below frost line in northern regions. The oval surface dimensions should be 12 x 20 inches. After digging the holes to proper depth for your locality, shovel gravel into the bottom to a 6-inch depth. See "Setting Posts," page 52.

The outer set of swing posts has two spacers, one near the middle and the other near the top, that will support the beam. The spacers are composed of 14½-inch lengths of scrap lumber, either three 2x4s for the triple 2x8 beam, or a 4x4 for a 4x8 beam. Only the middle spacer is installed at this point; the top spacer is installed after the posts are set in concrete. To position the middle spacer for the outer posts, insert one of the posts into the posthole, resting it on the 6 inches of gravel. Measure upward from the eventual level of the impact-reducing material 66 inches, and make a mark for the center of the middle spacer block, as shown. Lay the swing posts on a flat surface, and center the spacer on the mark; then temporarily clamp the assembly together.

Raise the doubled-swing posts in their hole, and brace them temporarily, as shown. Use string lines from the Central Tower to align the posts with the Central Tower, and ensure plumb, adjusting braces as necessary. Do not add concrete yet.

PREPARING THE BEAM

The ideal beam for the Swing Frame is a 14-foot 4x8. But 4x8s can be hard to find in many locales. And they can be quite heavy, especially if pressure treated and still wet.

The plans call for a built-up beam composed of three 2x8s bolted together. Structurally, two 2x8s are nearly as strong as a single 4x8 even though they are ½ inch thinner. Yet, by adding a third 2x8, you'll have solid wood for the drilling of eyebolt holes and other supporting hardware. Also, working with individual 2x8s is much easier on your back than working with a 4x8. The following instructions assume that you'll have a strong helper or two for lifting the beam into place. But if you work alone, you could instead position the 2x8s one at a time, and then clamp them together before drilling bolt holes.

The dimensions in the plans call for a 14-foot beam, and if you are careful in your measurements and construction, you can buy a 14 footer. We recommend, however, that you buy 16-foot boards, and cut them to finished length only after the Swing Frame is completed. That way, you won't need to worry that slightly out-of-place posts will leave you with a beam that is too short. Also, many lumberyards carry 2x8s in 12- and 16-, not 14-, foot lengths.

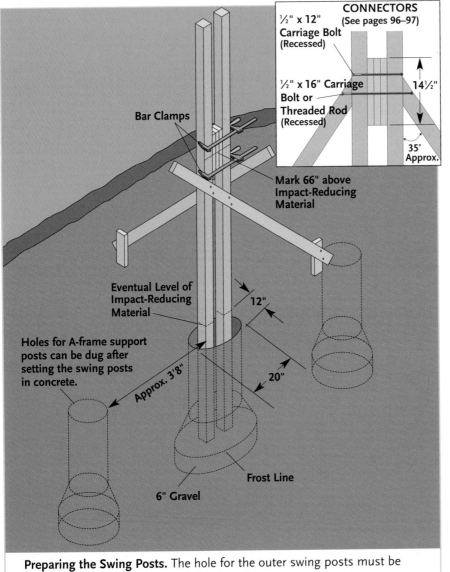

CONNECTORS (See pages 96–97)
½" x 12" Carriage Bolt (Recessed)
½" x 16" Carriage Bolt or Threaded Rod (Recessed)
14½"
35° Approx.

Bar Clamps

Mark 66" above Impact-Reducing Material

Eventual Level of Impact-Reducing Material

12"

Holes for A-frame support posts can be dug after setting the swing posts in concrete.

Approx. 3'8"

20"

6" Gravel

Frost Line

Preparing the Swing Posts. The hole for the outer swing posts must be wider for the double posts than for the A-frame support posts.

1 **Make a Built-up Beam.** On a level surface, clamp the three 2x8s together, with all sides and ends flush. Drill six 3/8-inch bolt holes, as shown. The two 1/2-inch holes on the left end will be used to attach the beam to post B1 on the Central Tower. Offset these holes slightly to minimize the chance of splitting the post. The 3/8-inch holes do not need to be offset, because they are not attached to posts. Insert and tighten the 3/8 x 5-inch bolts. Later, you will drill six more bolt holes for a swing-post attachment.

2 **Drill Holes for Eyebolts.** Next, lay out and drill holes for the eyebolts that will suspend the swings. The illustration allows recommended spacings between swings and posts, measured 48 inches above ground level, when swing chain tapers inward toward the seat. Tapered swing chains are safer; they help keep the swing moving in intended back-and-forth arcs. The dimensions given are suitable for most commercial swing seats, but consult the manufacturer before drilling.

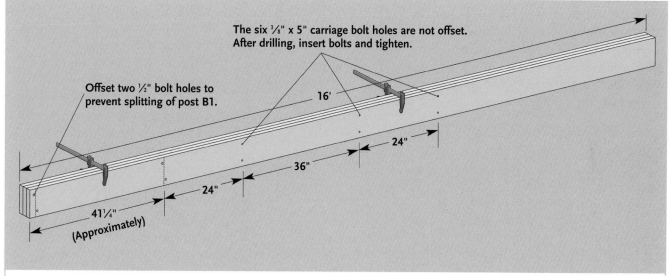

1 **To make a built-up beam,** bolt the three 2x8s together at their midsection with six 3/8-in. carriage bolts. The 41 1/2-in. spacing for the four eventual 1/2-in. bolts at the Central Tower is approximated here; drill only the two holes shown.

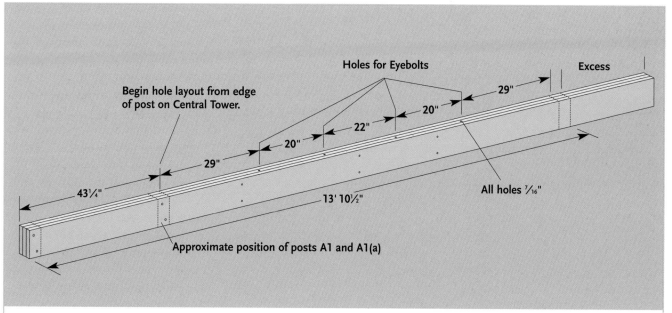

2 **To drill holes for eyebolts,** center the holes on the middle beam, allowing the spacing shown. This spacing is recommended by the U.S. Consumer Products Safety Commission to ensure safe distances between swings and posts.

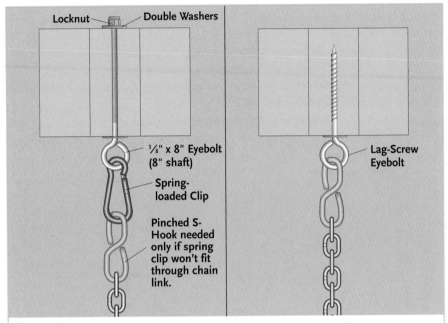

Locknut — Double Washers

³⁄₈" x 8" Eyebolt (8" shaft)

Spring-loaded Clip

Pinched S-Hook needed only if spring clip won't fit through chain link.

Lag-Screw Eyebolt

3 **Install the hardware.** Secure the eyebolts with double washers and a locknut on top of the beam. Because eyebolts will bear more weight than lag screws, lag screws should be used only for light loads, such as toddler swings. Use spring-loaded clips and S-hooks to attach the chain.

3 **Install the Hardware.** The plans call for using ³⁄₈ x 8-inch eyebolts. Be aware that different manufacturers measure eyebolt lengths differently. For some, the 8-inch dimension is an overall length, while for others the 8-inch length refers to the shaft below the eye. Look for eyebolts with at least an 8-inch shaft. One possible alternative for a light-duty toddler swing is ³⁄₈-inch lag-screw eyebolts, shown on the next page.

For the ³⁄₈-inch eyebolts, drill ⁷⁄₁₆-inch holes as straight as possible through the middle board in the beam. Attach the eyebolts with double washers on top and a single washer on the bottom, as shown, fastening them with ³⁄₈-inch locknuts.

INSTALLING THE BEAM

At the Central Tower, on the three posts that will support the swing, measure and mark 36 inches up from the upper deck surface. The bottom of

the swing beam will align with these marks. With a helper or two, raise the beam into position using the temporary cleats shown as supports. When the beam is aligned with the layout mark on post A1, adjust the ends for level; then clamp the beam at each end. (At the outer posts, clamp the beam to only one post, not both. Otherwise, the temporary cleat would prevent a tight "sandwiching" of the beam between posts.)

At the outer posts, drill two offset ¹⁄₂-inch holes through posts and beam, drilling recesses on the second post. (See "Recessing Hardware," page 80.) Install ¹⁄₂ x 12-inch carriage bolts, and tighten the nuts.

At post B1 on the Central Tower, use the beam's two ¹⁄₂-inch holes as guides to continue the holes through the post, drilling recesses on the back-side of the post before installing bolts and nuts.

At post A1(a), remove the temporary cleat and drill two offset ¹⁄₂-inch holes through the posts and beam.

Drill recesses on the backside of A1 before installing bolts and nuts.

Back at the outer posts, remove the temporary cleat. Then clamp, drill, recess, and bolt the top spacer, shown right, so that it is flush with the bottom of the beam.

Recheck that the outer swing posts are plumb. Then fill the posthole with concrete to 3 inches below grade, sloping the concrete's surface away from the posts to promote rain runoff. Let the concrete cure overnight, and do not allow anyone to use the Central Tower during that time.

Dig postholes for the A-frame; attach the supports as shown on page 98, and fill the holes with concrete to 3 inches below grade.

INSTALLING THE SWINGS

In addition to the seat and chain, each swing requires two ³⁄₈ x 3¹⁄₂-inch spring-loaded clips. If you have clips, you would need S-hooks here only if the clips won't fit through small chain links. With large pliers, close the ends of the S-hooks tightly so that they cannot slip off the clips or chain. If you can't close the S-hooks with large pliers, remove the clips from the eyebolts, and use a hammer or a vise to close them. Attach the seats to the chain with S-hooks (also closing them) or as directed by the manufacturer.

Ensure that the eyes of the eyebolts are perpendicular to the length of the beam, as shown. Proper position of all hardware will provide the best swinging motion.

Install swing seats just low enough so your children's feet can touch the ground (14 to 18 inches is usually ideal). You can add extra sets of S-hooks in the chain, and then close them to allow easy raising or lowering of the seat by means of the spring-loaded clips. Be sure to close the S-hooks completely.

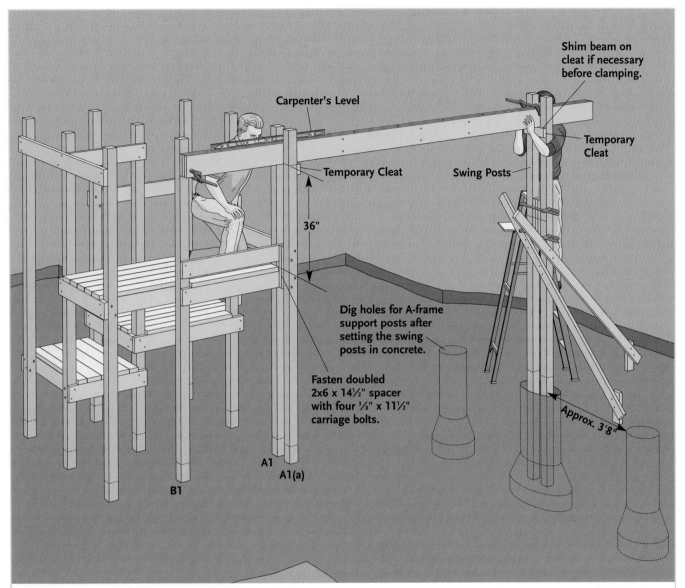

Installing the Beam. Rest the beam on temporary cleats before leveling and clamping the beam at its intended position. Ensure that you have enough strong help, and begin by hoisting the tower end of the beam to the person atop the tower.

SWING SUBSTITUTES

You can also use the installed eyebolts to suspend rings or a 20-inch trapeze bar, a commonly available size. For the quick switches of accessories, attach the proper length of chain for each with closed S-hooks. Then simply remove each by means of spring-loaded clips.

For a tire swing, use only a swivel manufactured specifically for that purpose. Attach the swivel to the beam, centering it between the posts. Install the tire so its bottom is at least 2 feet above the ground.

Swings take a beating, and their hardware gets stressed. On a regular basis, inspect all hardware, and replace parts that are worn or rusting. Especially check the nuts that secure eyebolts, and tighten or replace as needed.

Caution: The U.S. Consumer Product Safety Commission considers trapeze bars and exercise rings to be athletic equipment and does not recommend them for playgrounds. If you install such equipment, be cautioned that it allows children to turn themselves upside down, increasing the chances for head-first falls.

As for a tire swing, because it can rotate in all directions, avoid installing it where it could impact support posts or another swing apparatus. At the very least, ensure that there's extra-thick reduced-impact material wherever swing arcs could project a child. As this area becomes compressed with use and weather, refresh it regularly.

STAND-ALONE SWING FRAME

To construct a stand-alone Swing Frame, you need to set double 4x4 posts in concrete on both sides. Then follow instructions here. (You can build a double Swing Frame by using the heftier beam and bolt sizes indicated with earlier instructions.)

Dig two 12 x 20-inch postholes to at least three feet, plus at least 6 inches below frost line in northern regions. Insert the 4x4 middle spacers, and then place both sets of posts in the holes. When the posts are spaced properly and plumb, brace them securely.

Measure up one post 8 feet above the eventual surface of impact-reducing material, and mark. Using a line level or a carpenter's level on a long straight board, transfer this mark to the other set of posts. Install the top spacers, with their tops aligned with the marks.

Lay out the beam for the eyebolt positions, as shown right. Drill $7/16$-inch holes for the eyebolts and install the eyebolts with double washers on top, a single washer on the bottom, and locknuts.

Lift the beam into position, resting it on the top spacers. Check once again that the beam is level. (If it isn't, place shims between the beam and one spacer.) Drill holes through posts and beams for the $1/2$-inch carriage bolts. Install and tighten the bolts, washers, and nuts.

Fill the holes with concrete to 3 inches below ground level, sloping the surface away from the posts. Leave the bracing in place overnight while the concrete cures.

Attach the swings as described on page 96. Dig the four holes for the A-frame. Pour concrete into the holes to about 5 inches below ground level. Then proceed as shown at right.

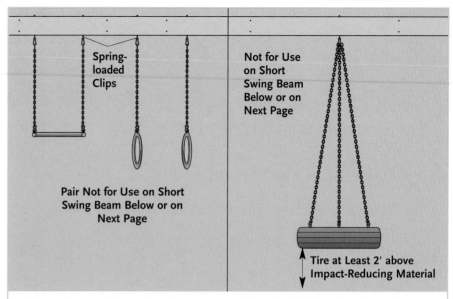

Spring-loaded Clips

Pair Not for Use on Short Swing Beam Below or on Next Page

Not for Use on Short Swing Beam Below or on Next Page

Tire at Least 2' above Impact-Reducing Material

Trapeze bars and exercise rings are considered athletic, rather than playground, equipment. They pose additional risk of headfirst falls. Because a tire swings in all directions, it should be the only swing suspended from the beam at one time.

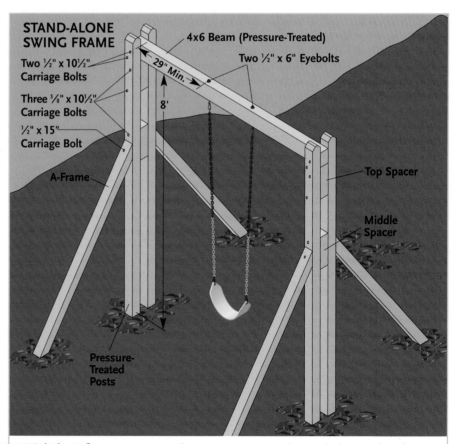

STAND-ALONE SWING FRAME

4x6 Beam (Pressure-Treated)

Two $1/2$" x $10 1/2$" Carriage Bolts

Two $1/2$" x 6" Eyebolts

Three $3/8$" x $10 1/2$" Carriage Bolts

$1/2$" x 15" Carriage Bolt

29" Min.

8'

A-Frame

Top Spacer

Middle Spacer

Pressure-Treated Posts

Sink the A-frame posts into the wet concrete so the angled tops abut the swing posts exactly opposite each other. Drill through the assembly, securing it with a $1/2$ x 15-in. carriage bolt or threaded rod, first recessing for washers and nuts.

SWING FRAME FOR A SINGLE SWING

If all you need—or have room for—is a single swing, the accompanying illustration gives the necessary dimensions and materials. Use a 12-foot 4x6 for the swing beam. You can cut it to finished length after installation. Make the three 12-inch spacers from scrap 4x4s. Note that because the 4x6 beam for a single swing is an inch thinner than the built-up beam for the double swing, bolt lengths must be shortened accordingly.

This Swing Frame will also accommodate a single trapeze bar or a set of rings. But it is not wide enough for a tire swing, which swings in all directions. (See "Caution" on trapeze bars and exercise rings on page 97.)

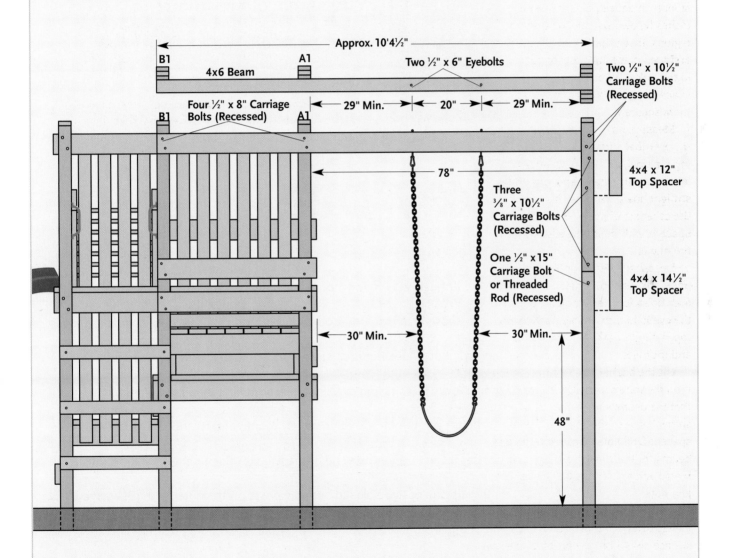

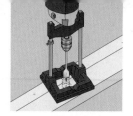

8 monkey bar

Although kids love whooshing down a slide and "flying" on a swing, those activities don't offer much physical challenge. A monkey bar is fun, too, but it also requires strenuous effort that develops strength and co-ordination. Thus, it is an excellent component for the Kids' Playland.

Better yet, the Monkey Bar is easy to add and to afford. Two posts on the Central Tower support one end of the Monkey Bar, so the only strenuous work is the digging of two holes to support posts on the outer end. (See page 107.)

The plans show a sloping monkey bar, descending from 84 inches at the Central Tower to 60 inches at the outer end. This is a good height for most kids 6 years and older. The slope makes the bars more of a challenge ascend-ing than descending. For younger kids install the bar lower, so that they can reach the bar nearest the Tower without jumping.

BAR VANTAGES

The bar slope shown is optional. Feel free to instead install horizontal bars at a lower height for children younger than 6 years or so.

The first bar nearest the Central Tower is set some distance from the posts. This is an important safety feature—don't place the first bar directly over the platform at the Tower. Children should need to reach out to grasp the first bar. That way, should they fall, they on the impact-reducing material and not against the platform. The ground beneath should be covered with extra-thick impact-reducing material, which you should maintain regularly.

For individual bars themselves, we recommend hardwood dowels, although you could use galvanized pipe. The biggest advantage of wood dowels is that they won't become too cold or too hot in extreme weather. Wood is also more comfortable to grasp in any weather.

If you use plumbing pipe, or a thicker dowel, be sure to drill mounting holes to match their diameter. The best diameters for dowels are 1 to 1½ inches. Larger diameters are hard for children to grasp.

LAYING OUT POSTHOLES

If you didn't mark the Monkey Bar postholes when laying out the Playland initially, set the two 2x6 rails on the ground, on edge and with their ends flush with the back edges of the Central Tower posts, as shown opposite. If necessary, temporarily fasten the rails to the posts to hold the rails upright. On the outer end, adjust the rails so that their outside faces are exactly 24 inches apart, also squaring them with the near wall of the Central Tower.

Measure back on each rail 6 inches,

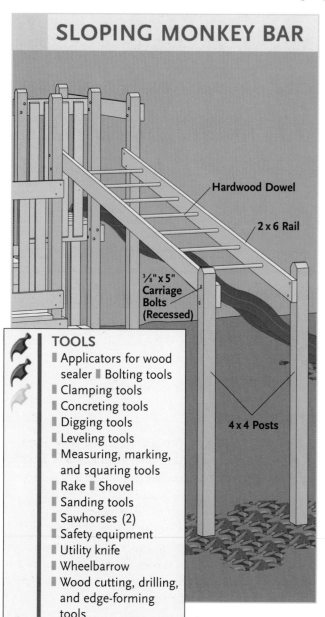

SLOPING MONKEY BAR

Hardwood Dowel

2 x 6 Rail

⅜" x 5" Carriage Bolts (Recessed)

4 x 4 Posts

TOOLS
- Applicators for wood sealer
- Bolting tools
- Clamping tools
- Concreting tools
- Digging tools
- Leveling tools
- Measuring, marking, and squaring tools
- Rake
- Shovel
- Sanding tools
- Sawhorses (2)
- Safety equipment
- Utility knife
- Wheelbarrow
- Wood cutting, drilling, and edge-forming tools

lumber and materials order

LUMBER

Lumber	Quantity	Size
4x4s	2	10' minimum
2x6s	2	10'
Hardwood dowels	4	1" x 4'

HARDWARE AND MORE

Materials	Quantity	Size
Decking screws	14	3"
Carriage bolts, washers, and nuts	8	⅜" x 5"
Concrete		
Gravel		
Construction adhesive or polyurethene glue		
Impact-reducing material		
Finish		

CUTTING LIST

Materials	Quantity	Size
Dowels	7	22½"

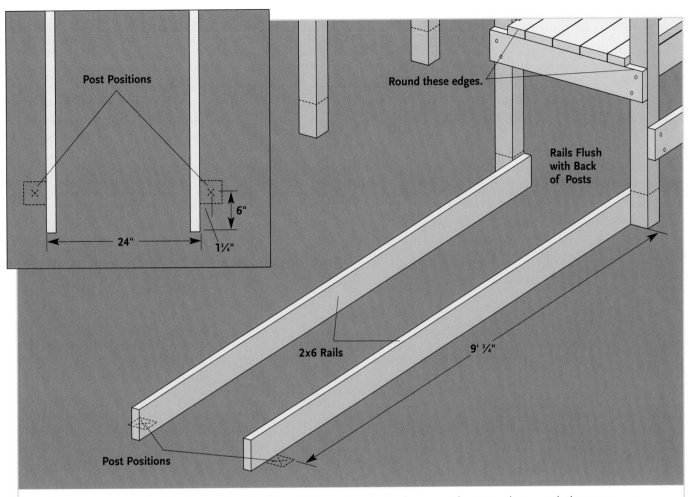

Laying Out Post Holes. With posts for the Central Tower already in place, use the 2x6 rails to mark the post locations for the Monkey Bar.

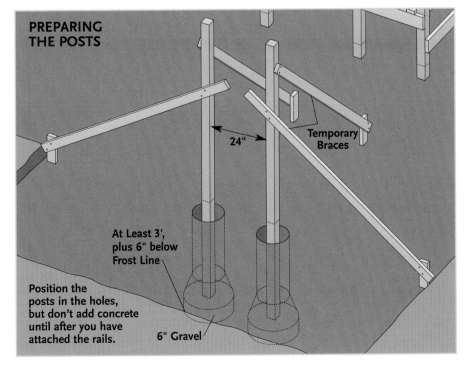

then out 1¾ inches, as shown. These locations will be the centers of the two new postholes. Mark them with a small piece of wood. Remove the rails, and set them aside.

PREPARING THE POSTS

Dig the two postholes to at least 3 feet and an additional 6 inches below frost line in northern regions. (See "Setting Posts" on page 52 for more on posthole digging.) Set the posts in the holes, 24 inches apart and 9 feet ¾ inch from the posts on the Central Tower, as shown. Plumb the posts, and brace them securely, but do not fill the holes with concrete yet.

BUILDING THE BAR

The bar is assembled by inserting dowels into matching holes drilled halfway into the face of each rail. The dowels are held in place with glue and screws. The dimensions given here assume that spacing between posts on each end of the Monkey Bar is exactly 24 inches. If this spacing is off by even a fraction of an inch—and don't be surprised if it is—now is the time to determine it and make necessary adjustments.

1 **Check the Post Spacing.** At the Central Tower, measure from the decking surface up each post 60 inches, or a lesser height, and make a mark at that spot. Now carefully measure the distance between the posts at the mark. If it is exactly 24 inches, you can proceed with the instructions exactly as given.

If the spacing between posts is a bit over or under 24 inches, cut the dowels to a length that makes up the difference. For example, if the spacing is 23½ inches, subtract ½ inch from the dowel length. In this case, your dowels would be 22 inches long. Likewise, for example, if the spacing between posts is 24¾ inches, you would cut dowels 23¼ inches long. This is the only adjustment necessary to ensure that the bars fit snugly between the posts. You can cut one dowel and use it as a template for the rest.

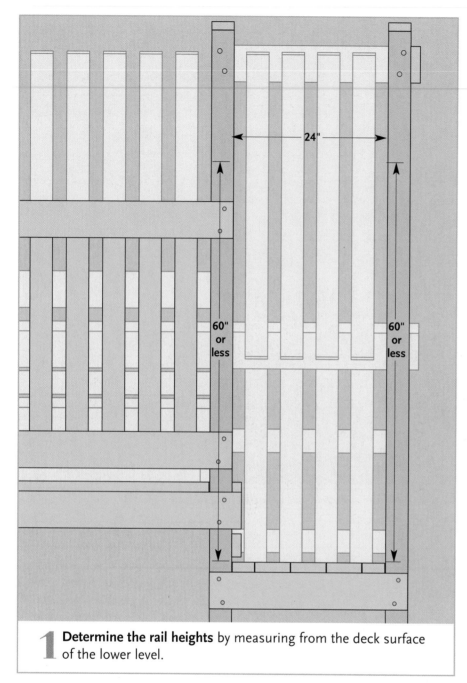

1 **Determine the rail heights** by measuring from the deck surface of the lower level.

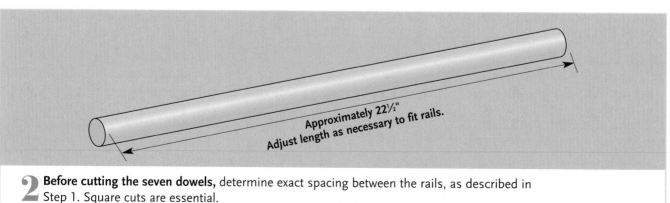

Approximately 22½"
Adjust length as necessary to fit rails.

2 **Before cutting the seven dowels,** determine exact spacing between the rails, as described in Step 1. Square cuts are essential.

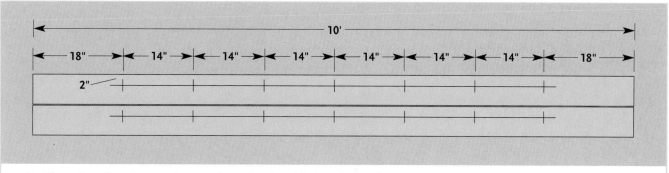

3 **Place the rails edge to edge,** marking the dowel holes identically on each.

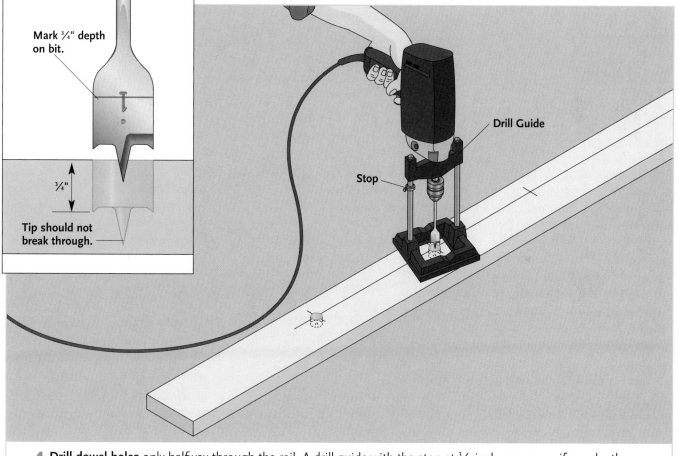

Mark ¾" depth on bit.

¾"

Tip should not break through.

Drill Guide

Stop

4 **Drill dowel holes** only halfway through the rail. A drill guide with the stop at ¾ inch ensures uniform depths.

2 **Cut the Dowels.** Cut a total of seven dowels to a length of 22½ inches or the length calculated in the previous step. For best results, make the cuts as square as possible. A table saw or power miter saw will produce the most accurate results. If you must use a hand saw, take a little extra time to produce the squarest ends you can.

3 **Prepare the Rails.** Lay both 2x6 rails on a flat surface. On the inside face of each, mark a layout line along the length of the board 2 inches from the top edge. Now mark the dowel hole layout along this line, 18 inches from the end of each board and then every 14 inches on center. Measure and mark both rails at once.

4 **Drill the Dowel Holes.** On each board, drill 1-inch-diameter holes exactly ¾ inch deep. Ensure that the tip of your wood-boring bit won't break through the outside face of the board. The best way to control the depth of each hole is to use a drill press or a drill guide with the stop set for a ¾-inch depth. If you don't have access to either of these, mark the bit using a marker, and drill carefully.

5 Attach the Rails and Dowels. Spread a small amount of exterior glue around each dowel hole on one rail. Insert dowels into each hole, giving them a light tap with a hammer if necessary. Then apply glue to the dowel holes on the other rail, and fit the rail over the dowels.

After you have joined all dowels and rails, drill deck-screw pilot holes 3 inches deep through the top of the rails at each dowel location, $^3/_8$ inch from the inside edge. Then finish the assembly by driving 3-inch deck screws into each pilot hole.

ASSEMBLING THE MONKEY BAR

Attach the bar temporarily to the posts. If you like, adjust the height of the bar at either end to suit the needs of your children. Mark cutoff lines on the rails and posts. Then take the bar down, and make the cuts.

1 Mark the End Posts. Measure up one end post 60 inches, or to a lower height for kids 6 years and younger, and make a mark. Using a level, transfer this mark to the other post.

2 Temporarily Attach the Bar. With a helper, raise the rails between the posts. Center the rails on the height marks you made on the end posts and the marks you made earlier on the posts at the Central Tower (60 inches or less above the deck). Temporarily attach the rails to the posts using clamps or screws.

Check the end posts for plumb, and make adjustments as necessary. Pour concrete into the holes to 3 inches below ground level, tapering the surface of the concrete away from the posts. Let the concrete cure undisturbed overnight. Then top off the holes with dirt.

Mark and cut off the rails at the end

posts, using the posts as a guide. At this time you can either cut off the end posts at the tops of rails or leave them long enough to allow your raising the rails as your kids grow taller.

Remove the bar and make all of the necessary cuts. Round-over and smooth all sharp or rough edges.

3 Permanently Attach the Bar. Clamp or temporarily screw the bar to the

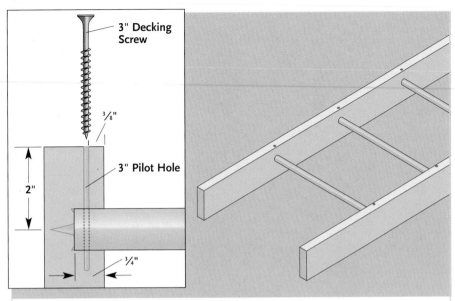

5 Attach the Rails and Dowels. Use glue and screws to fasten the dowels to the rails.

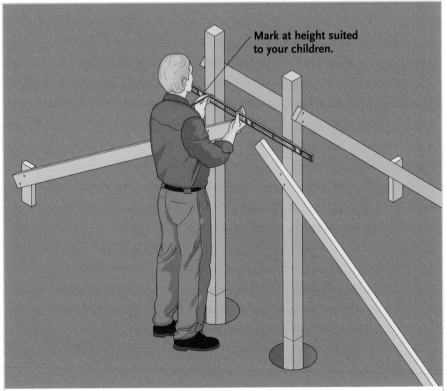

Mark at height suited to your children.

1 At a rail height suitable for your children, use a level to extend the reference line to the second post.

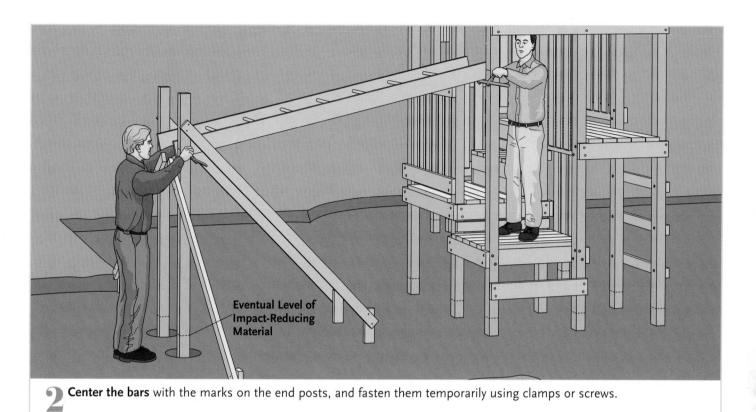

2 **Center the bars** with the marks on the end posts, and fasten them temporarily using clamps or screws.

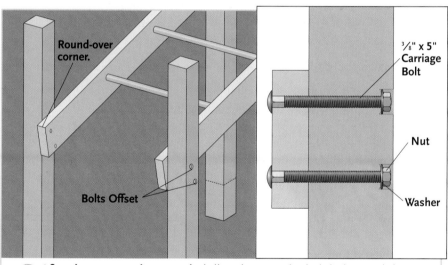

Round-over corner.

Bolts Offset

$\frac{3}{8}$" x 5" Carriage Bolt

Nut

Washer

3 **After the concrete has cured,** drill and recess the bolt holes, and then fasten the bars to the posts.

posts. Drill two $\frac{3}{8}$-inch holes through each rail and post junction, offsetting them so they don't split the posts. Drill $\frac{1}{2}$-inch deep recesses on the outsides of the posts, as shown. Fasten with 5-inch carriage bolts, washers, and nuts.

4 **Create a Launch Pad.** Rather than adding a wood step on the end posts to allow smaller kids to reach the

first dowel, lay a 24-inch-diameter truck tire (not shown) flat between the posts and fill it with impact-reducing material, after roping the tire to the posts on each side. This lets smaller kids reach the first bar, and it provides a cushioned landing pad when kids descend from the Tower end. Remove the tire after your kids outgrow the need.

4 **For a step** to help smaller kids reach the first bar, we recommend a 24-in.-diameter truck tire (not shown) filled with impact-reducing material.

107

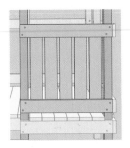

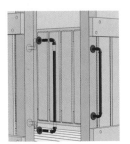

9 playhouse

The Playhouse has something for everyone. For kids, it offers an elevated, covered, and reasonably private outdoor room that can serve a range of functions from clubhouse to quiet haven. For parents, the Playhouse offers most of the attractions of a tree house, but without the combined dangers of height and structural uncertainty. Besides, the Playhouse need not be so private that younger kids are completely hidden from view, and it is reasonably easy to construct.

The plans call for a deck surface only 20 inches above ground. Because the deck is low, the ground beneath the Playhouse doesn't require special impact-reducing material. The low profile also means that the Playhouse can be built without need to bury posts in concrete. With bolts and screws for most of the joinery, this structure can be dismantled easily when it has outlived its purpose.

PREPARING THE SITE

The Playhouse can be placed directly on grass. But a better approach might be to remove the sod beneath the structure; lay down some landscape fabric; and then fill the excavation with gravel. Because the grass will probably die from lack of sunlight anyway, gravel will be more attractive than bare ground. Additionally, this impact-reducing material will help as you level the structure, and it will prevent water

from pooling beneath it.

Because you don't need to dig post-holes for this project, layout steps are simpler than those for the Kids' Playland. Nor is it necessary to rely on batter boards and strings to keep the sides properly aligned.

The basic plans for the playhouse show a relatively low deck height. This offers several advantages: it eliminates concerns about kids falling from great heights to the ground; posts don't need to be braced or buried in concrete; and kids usually won't mind that

their Playhouse isn't higher. If you prefer to build the deck a little higher, you can do so following essentially the same design. But with a deck height of more than 20 inches, up to about 36 inches, you should add 2x6 base supports and 2x4 cross bracing all around, as shown on page 123, as well as at least 6 inches of impact-reducing material under the doorway and around the entire structure.

If you want a deck higher than 36 inches, embed the posts in concrete. For that, see "Setting Posts," page 52.

PLAYHOUSE WITH ROOF OF BEVELED SIDING

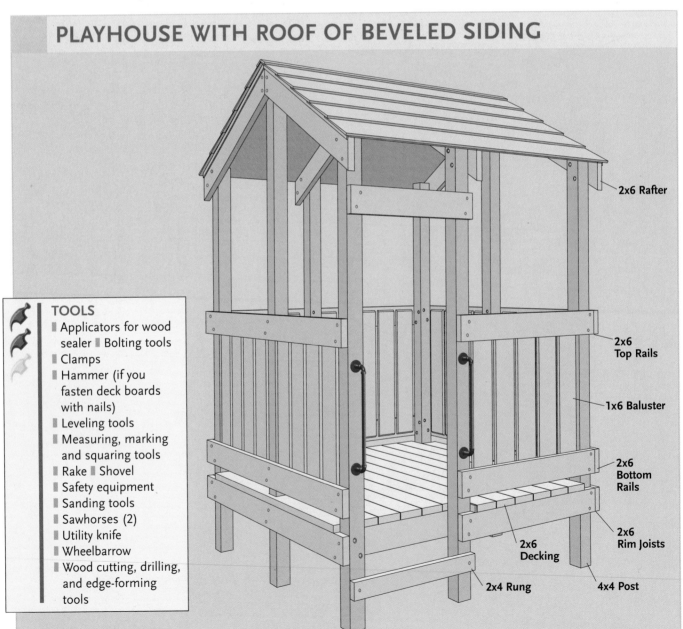

TOOLS
- Applicators for wood sealer ▌ Bolting tools
- Clamps
- Hammer (if you fasten deck boards with nails)
- Leveling tools
- Measuring, marking and squaring tools
- Rake ▌ Shovel
- Safety equipment
- Sanding tools
- Sawhorses (2)
- Utility knife
- Wheelbarrow
- Wood cutting, drilling, and edge-forming tools

2x6 Rafter

2x6 Top Rails

1x6 Baluster

2x6 Bottom Rails

2x6 Rim Joists

2x6 Decking

2x4 Rung

4x4 Post

PREPARING THE LUMBER

It is easier to do the bulk of smoothing and sanding of lumber before construction begins. With the right power tools, this step can be relatively quick and simple. First, round-over the edges of the posts and the top edge of the top rails using a router equipped with a roundover bit. Then smooth all exposed surfaces using a power sander, removing any mill stamps on the lumber as you go. In addition to providing a surface that is friendlier to small hands, the sanded wood will better absorb the finish you apply later.

Use a router with roundover bit, as shown, or a belt sander to soften edges and corners that kids might accidentally bump into.

lumber, materials, and cutting list

LUMBER AND MATERIALS ORDER

Lumber	Quantity	Size
4x4s (pressure-treated posts)	6	8'
	2	10'
2x6s (joists, rails, rafters, ridge)	15	12'
	4	8'
2x4s (step)	1	8'
1x6s (balusters)	10	10'
Roof covering (choose among options)		@ 50 sq. ft.

HARDWARE AND MORE

Lumber	Quantity	Size
Carriage bolts, nuts, and washers	14	$\frac{3}{8}$" x 7"
	12	$\frac{3}{8}$" x 5$\frac{1}{2}$"
	62	$\frac{3}{8}$" x 5"
Lag screws	8	$\frac{5}{16}$" x 4"
2x6 joist hangers and nails	2	
Deck screws	200	3"
	150	2$\frac{1}{2}$"
Finish		

CUTTING LIST

	Quantity	Size
Posts	2	4x4 9'6"
Joists	1	2x6 70"
	1	2x6 68$\frac{1}{2}$"
	5	2x6 69"
	1	2x6 41$\frac{1}{2}$"
Rung	1	2x4 31"
Door header	1	2x6 31"
Decking	5	2x6 65"
	8	2x6 70"
Top/Bottom rails	2	2x6 70"
	2	2x6 41$\frac{1}{2}$"
	2	2x6 69"
	2	2x6 68$\frac{1}{2}$"
Rafters	6	2x6 48"
Ridge	1	2x6 62"
Balusters	29	1x6 36"

BUILDING THE SIDEWALLS

The sidewalls (Sides B and D in the accompanying drawing) are virtually identical, except that the rim joist and both rails on Side D are 1½ inches longer. Study the illustrations to familiarize yourself with the details. As shown, each wall is assembled on the ground before being raised.

The four 4x4 corner posts should each be 8 feet long. From 10-foot 4x4s, cut the two center posts to 9 feet, 6 inches. Lay the posts on the ground, then measure from the bottom, and mark layout lines for the tops of the rim joist and two rails at 18½ inches, 27½ inches, and 60 inches, as shown. Space the posts 28¼ inches apart, making sure that the bottoms are in line.

Next, cut the rails and rim joists. Using 2x6s, cut three boards 70 inches long for Side D, and three others 68½ inches long for Side B. Place the cut 2x6s across the posts with their top edges aligned with the layout marks. Check that the boards for Side D overlap the outside posts by 1½ inches on each side; those for Side B should not overlap the corner "door post."

Mark the bolt-hole locations on each board. The bolts must be offset vertically on each post side and staggered to allow for bolting through adjacent sides of the post so that the bolts don't hit one another. See the section "Staggering Bolt Holes" on page 80 for detailed instructions. Temporarily fasten the boards to the posts with 3-inch screws that you will replace with bolts once the walls are raised. The holes left by the screws will serve as pilots for drilling the bolt holes, so take care to drive the screws as straight as possible.

Now cut the four outside rafters, using 48-inch 2x6s. To do this, lay one board across the tops of a center post and a corner post, with the top of the rafter flush with the edges of the posts, as shown. Use a sliding bevel gauge to

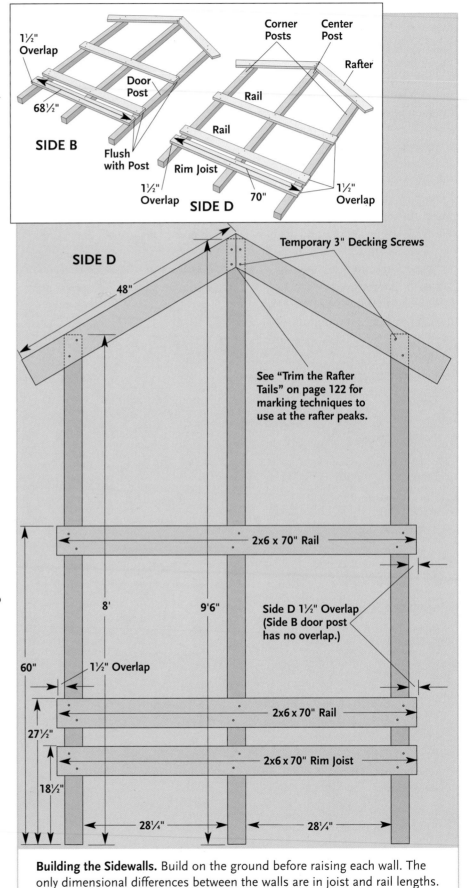

Building the Sidewalls. Build on the ground before raising each wall. The only dimensional differences between the walls are in joist and rail lengths.

determine the angle to plumb-cut the rafter peaks, about 60 degrees. (For marking savvy, see "Trim the Rafter Tail" on page 122.) Mark and cut the angle. Check the fit and alignment of each rafter. If the plumb cuts aren't perfectly in line, adjust your bevel gauge a few degrees. Mark and cut the remaining rafters, and fasten with screws.

RAISING THE SIDEWALLS

Cut seven 2x6s to 69-inch lengths. Five will serve as floor joists and two will serve as rails for the back wall. Mark the bolt-hole locations on each board, again making certain that they are offset and staggered.

Carefully raise each wall into position, and brace each plumb and parallel with its opposite wall; alternatively, a couple of helpers could hold the walls in place. Temporarily attach the backside top rail with 3-inch screws. Then attach the outside joist on the back wall and the long joist on the inside of the posts on the front wall. With a helper or two, shift the walls until diagonal posts are equidistant, making the structure square. Level the structure by digging under posts or shimming them up, checking joists with a carpenter's level.

FRAMING THE FRONT WALL

Cut three 2x6s to 41½ inches to serve as the rails and outside joist on the front wall. Mark layout lines on a 4x4 post at the same distances from the bottom as on the other posts, as shown. With a helper, hold the inner door post upright while you drive temporary screws through the rails, ensuring that each board is flush with the outside edge of each post.

Now cut and attach the 2x6 door-way header and the 2x4 step.

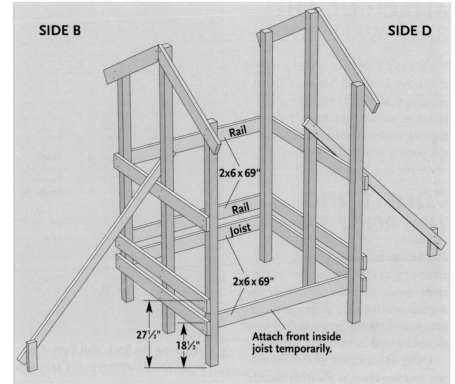

Raising the Sidewalls. After raising the side walls, temporarily attach rim joists and, for the back wall, rails as well.

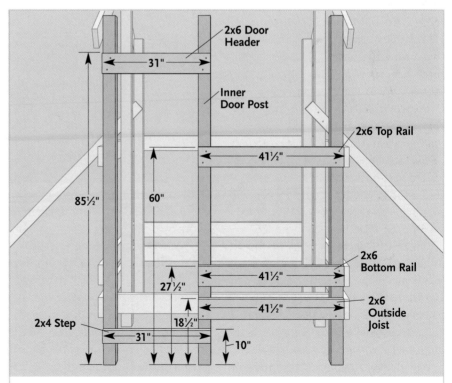

Framing the Front Wall. After marking layout lines as indicated on the posts, temporarily fasten the 41½-in. rails and joist to the inner door post. Then temporarily attach the 2x6 door header and 2x4 step.

FINAL TOUCHES

Finishing. Apply the finish of your choice. For advice on types of finishes, see Chapter 5, page 64.

Handbars. A couple of handbars in the doorway will make climbing into the Playhouse a little easier for most kids. For this you can use common galvanized plumbing materials to fashion large handbars. For each handbar you will need two ½-inch floor flanges; two 1-inch nipples; two 90-degree elbows; and about an 18-inch length of threaded

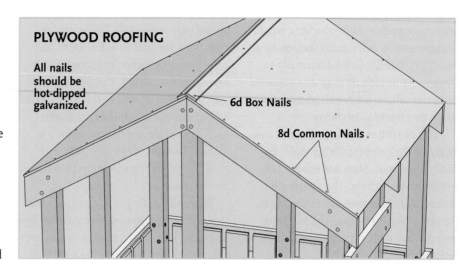

PLYWOOD ROOFING

All nails should be hot-dipped galvanized.

6d Box Nails

8d Common Nails

● TRIM THE RAFTER TAILS

The rafter tails will look better if you cut them plumb, although this step is optional. First decide how much you want the roof to overhang. Measure the amount of overhang horizontally from the post to the rafter, and mark each rafter. The illustration shows a 3-inch overhang.

To make a plumb cut at the end of each rafter, place the bevel gauge on top of the rafter, aligning the metal blade against the near post. Set the gauge's locking wing nut, and copy that angle to the overhang mark

where you wish to cut each rafter, thereby providing plumb cutting lines.

For a more finished look, you can conceal rafter ends by attaching a fascia board. Do this by cutting a 1x6 to span the rafters. Then align it by means of a framing square, as shown, so that the top of the fascia board doesn't project into roofing material yet to come. Drive three 6d nails or 2-inch decking screws through the fascia into each rafter.

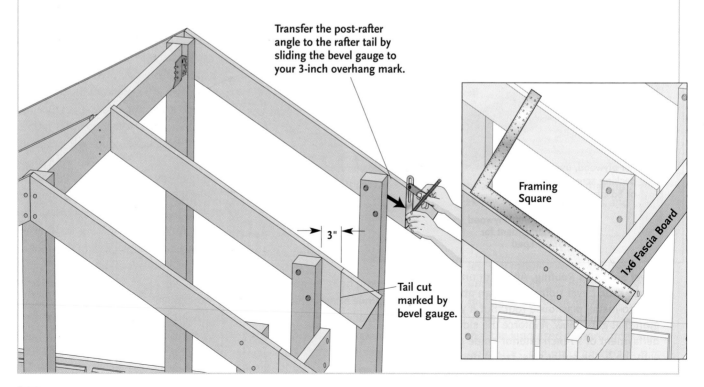

Transfer the post-rafter angle to the rafter tail by sliding the bevel gauge to your 3-inch overhang mark.

3"

Tail cut marked by bevel gauge.

Framing Square

1x6 Fascia Board

pipe. Thread the parts together, and then drive screws through the flanges into the posts on both sides of the doorway. For a touch of color, first removing the oily residue on the pipe with hot water and either household soap or automotive cleaner, and before installing the handbars, paint them with a metal or auto-body paint.

As options, playground stores and some home centers carry plastic handles for use on structures. You could also buy a pair of large garage-door or barn-door handles. All handles should be fastened with screws.

Customizing the Playhouse. For features such as clubhouse signs, flags, and flagpoles, try to involve your children. They will be more proud of a sign or flag that they created than something conceived and created completely by adults.

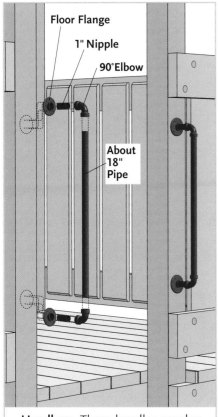

Handbars. These handles employ galvanized plumbing pipe and fittings, but commercial handles for play structures serve well too.

A TALLER PLAYHOUSE

If you prefer a somewhat higher deck, you can follow the same playhouse design on preceding pages. However, with a deck height of more than 20 inches, up to about 36 inches, you need to add 2x6 base supports and 2x4 cross bracing all around, as shown here. You should also add at least 6 inches of impact-reducing material around the entire structure, especially where kids are more likely to fall below the doorway.

123

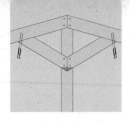

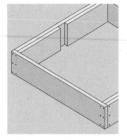

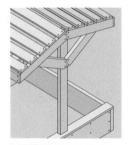

10 sandbox

Available almost everywhere, sand seems to attract people of all ages. Adults spend billions annually to visit sandy beaches, while children barely old enough to sit up can enjoy hours in the sand—shoveling, piling, and sifting.

Backyard sandboxes can stimulate creativity in children, whether for the building of sand castles or the construction of whole villages, complete with roads, traffic, and toy citizens. Sandboxes also promote cooperative play, helping teach children how to "build" toward a common goal.

A sandbox can be the simplest of all building projects. If you dig a shallow depression in the ground and fill it with sand, kids will find a way to have fun with it. The Sandbox featured here is covered to protect kids from the sun, providing a shady retreat for hours of play.

DESIGN OPTIONS

The covered Sandbox is moderately easy to construct, and requires a minimal amount of lumber. The roof is partly functional and partly decorative. It will block some sunlight but isn't intended to keep out rain. Perhaps more importantly, the roof lends a sense of enclosure that makes kids feel they have a space of their own. This sandbox is best suited to preschoolers. Once the kids grow tall enough to bump their heads on the roof, you can simply remove it. Cut the roof supports flush with the top of the seats, and round-over and sand sharp edges to prevent injury.

SITING AND OTHER BASICS

Try to position the Sandbox away from play components where there's more action. This makes sense first because sand play tends to be relatively stationary and quiet, but more importantly, for the sake of safety. To avoid mishaps, seated children should be isolated from those going full tilt. For example, never place a sandbox near a swingset or near the bottom of a slide with the intention of having it also serve as impact material there. Doing so would greatly increase the chances for collisions.

Also, a sandbox that is regularly exposed to direct sunlight will stay drier and will catch less falling debris than a sandbox under a tree.

Choosing the Sand. Sand is graded according to cleanliness and particle size. Home centers carry bags of sterilized "play sand," which is packaged in 40-pound bags for children's sandboxes. You can also use washed masonry sand, available at masonry supply outlets. It is often cheaper to buy sand by the truckload. Both play sand and masonry sand are fine-

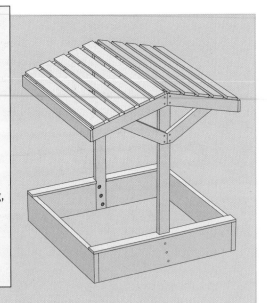

TOOLS
- Applicators for wood sealer
- Digging tools
- Leveling Tools
- Measuring, marking, and squaring tools
- Safety equipment
- Sanding tools
- Sawhorses (2)
- Utility knife
- Wood cutting, drilling, and edge-forming tools
- Bolting tools
- Clamps
- Hammer

lumber and materials order

LUMBER

Lumber	Quantity	Size
2x10	3	8'
2x4s	1	8'
	2	10'
1x4	8	8'

HARDWARE AND MORE

Materials	Quantity	Size
Deck screws	32	3"
	52	2½"
	64	1½"
Carriage bolts, nuts, and washers	6	⅜" x 3"
Sand	@10–12 cu. ft.	

CUTTING LIST

	Quantity	Size
Roof supports	2	2x4 54"
Rafters	4	2x4 25⅝"
Rafter braces	4	2x4 17¼"
Roof slats	10	1x4 48"
Fascia boards	2	1x4 48"
Box	2	2x10 48"
	2	2x10 45"
	4	2x10 20¾"
Seat	2	1x4 48"
	2	1x4 41"
Plastic mesh (to cover sand)	1	42" x 42"

grained, which is often preferred for sandbox play because it holds together better when wet.

However, sand with slightly larger particles has some advantages. It is less likely to penetrate clothing and so get carried into the house. It won't blow away as easily, and it won't as readily clog up moving parts of toy tractors and trucks. Regardless of grain size, the important thing is that the sand be washed free of all organic materials, such as silt and clay.

For best results, the sand should be at least 8 to 10 inches deep, which is the minimum for "serious" digging. Deeper is better, up to about 20 inches. This depth also allows you or the kids to bring wetter sand up to the surface for modeling.

Construction Details. Any wood that will be in contact with ground or sand should be pressure treated or from a rot-resistant species. If you use untreated wood for the seats, round the edges and sand the wood relatively smooth before sealing it. Also ensure that no fasteners protrude.

Maintaining the Sandbox. Whether the Sandbox is covered or not, rake it regularly, and remove any debris. If the sand stays wet much of the time, raking will help dry it. Also, make a rule that there's to be no glass and no sharp metal, such as nails, used near the Sandbox. If glass gets broken and worked into the sand, replace all of the sand.

If the sand hasn't been used for a long time and seems dirty, consider replacing it.

COVERED SANDBOX

1 **Build the Roof Frame.** Use 2x4s for all parts of the roof frame. Vertical roof supports tie the sandbox to the roof. Rafters provide a fastening surface for the roofing slats, and braces strengthen the entire frame.

The two roof supports are 54 inches long. Make 15-degree angle cuts on both sides to form the peak. Or cut the posts after installing the rafters.

The four rafters are 25⅝-inches long. Make parallel 15-degree plumb cuts on both ends.

To make the four braces, start with 17¼-inch 2x4s. Make a 45-degree angle cut on the upper end, which will join the rafter, and a 30-degree cut on the lower end, which will connect with the roof support. Place each pair of cut

braces together as intended to meet. Draw a horizontal line about 1 inch up from the bottom point, as shown. Cut the braces along this line.

On a flat surface, lay the rafters and braces on each support. Check for a good fit between all pieces. Then fasten rafters and braces to the support by driving 2½-inch deck screws through the face of each. Attach the braces to the bottom of the rafters by driving 3-inch deck screws up through the bottom of the brace.

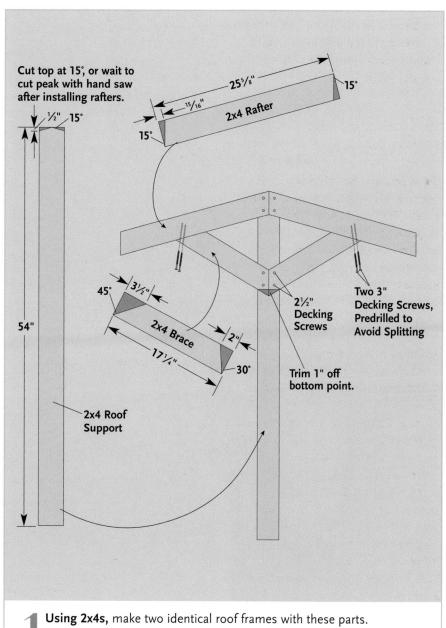

1 **Using 2x4s,** make two identical roof frames with these parts.

2 Build the Box. Use 2x10s to build the box for the sand. Cut two pieces to 48 inches each, two to 45 inches, and four to 20¾ inches.

Assemble the box as shown using 3-inch and 2½-inch deck screws. Make certain that none of the screws breaks through the wood on either side of the box.

3 Join the Roof Frame and Box. With the box resting on a flat surface, set one of the roof supports in the gap between the 2x10s inside the box. The support should fit snugly, but use a framing square to check the alignment. Clamp the support in place. Then drill three bolt holes through the box and support, offsetting the holes as shown to avoid splitting the wood. Then drill recess holes on the inside of the support, and fasten with ⅜ x 3-inch carriage bolts and recessed washers and nuts. Repeat with the other support.

4 Finish the Roof. Measure the span from the outside faces of the rafters. If it varies from 48 inches, be sure to cut slats and fascia boards to that length.

The number of slats and the size of the gap between them are up to you.

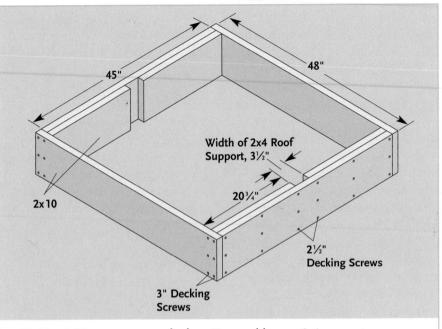

2 Use 2x10s to construct the box. You could use a 2x4 spacer to ensure that the inside gap is wide enough for the roof supports.

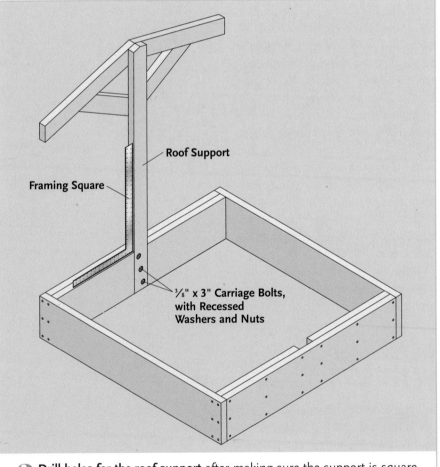

3 Drill holes for the roof support after making sure the support is square.

After construction, round-over all sharp corners and edges.

Our drawings show five 1x4 slats on each side of the roof, which allows for a gap of about 1½ inches between each board. Round-over the edges of the 1x4s. Then fasten the slats and fascia boards to the rafters with 1½ inch deck screws.

5 Attach the Seat, and Finish Up.
Adding a separate seat of untreated lumber is probably a good safety precaution if you used pressure-treated lumber for the box itself. And the 1x4s add some width to the sitting area. Round-over the edges of the 1x4s. Cut notches to fit around the roof supports, and fasten the seats with 1½-inch deck screws spaced about 6 inches apart.

Apply the finish of your choice to the Sandbox. Then fill it with sand, and let the kids dig in.

● COVERING THE SANDBOX

If your sandbox becomes a litter box for cats, you will need to cover it when not in use. A small plastic tarp held in place by a few bricks or large stones may be effective but unsightly. The better way to keep unwanted critters out is to use the plastic mesh shown below. This cover keeps cats out, yet allows the sand to dry after rain. Plastic mesh of 2" x 2" or smaller is available through garden suppliers.

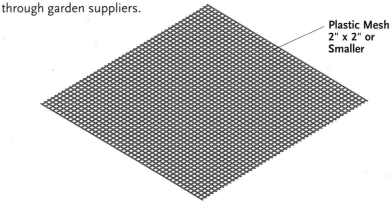

Plastic Mesh 2" x 2" or Smaller

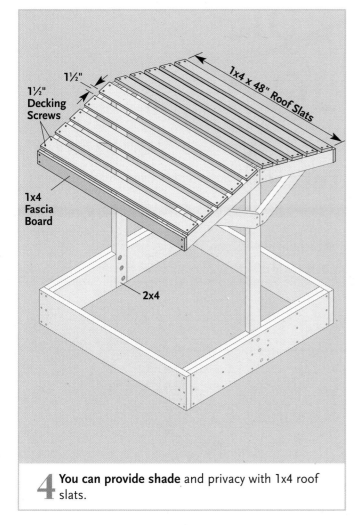

1½"

1½" Decking Screws

1x4 x 48" Roof Slats

1x4 Fascia Board

2x4

4 You can provide shade and privacy with 1x4 roof slats.

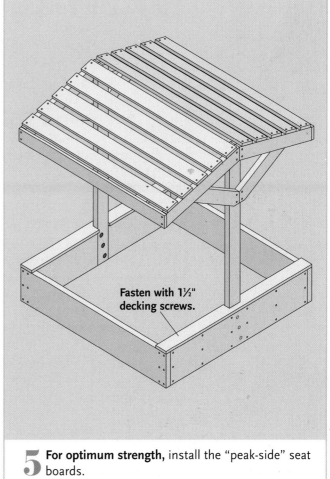

Fasten with 1½" decking screws.

5 For optimum strength, install the "peak-side" seat boards.

129

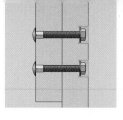

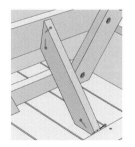

11 picnic table

This traditional A-framed picnic table is scaled down for children, yet it is sturdy and durable. Although most children will find the table height ideal, the table isn't so low that adults couldn't sit comfortably. Made from standard 2x4 and 2x6 lumber, this project requires a minimal cutting. Carriage bolts and screws accomplish all joinery.

You can build the picnic table from woods that are durable outdoors, whether pressure-treated lumber, cedar, or redwood, such as the table shown in the photo. Yet because the legs are in contact with the ground, pressure-treated lumber for the legs, at least, would be more durable. Regardless of the wood used, you should treat it with a semitransparent, water-repellent stain. Should the seat and tabletop begin to weather, they can be sanded and refinished. Or if they eventually show some rot, they can easily be replaced.

ASSEMBLING THE FRAME

The two identical A-shaped end braces are composed of 2x6 seat supports, 2x4 tabletop supports, and 2x6 legs. The four legs are from 32-inch-long 2x6s cut to 60 degrees at each end, as shown.

Working on a flat surface, lay the legs so that their outside corners are 52¼ inches apart at the bottom and 23½ inches apart at the top. Center the table-top support flush with the top edges of the legs and the seat support 9½ inches above the bottoms of the legs. When all of the pieces are in place and centered, drill ⅛-inch pilot holes through the supports and legs. Use the pilot holes as guides to drill the recesses for the bolts and washers on the insides of the legs. A 1⅛-inch-diameter recess, drilled ½-inch deep, should suffice, but measure your washers first to be sure they match the intended recess diameter.

Place the supports back on the legs, using the ⅛-inch drill bit to position them properly. Drill ⅜-inch holes through the supports and legs. After drilling each hole, insert a ⅜-inch carriage bolt, washer, and nut. This will keep the pieces in alignment while you drill the next hole. When all the bolts are in place, tighten the nuts securely.

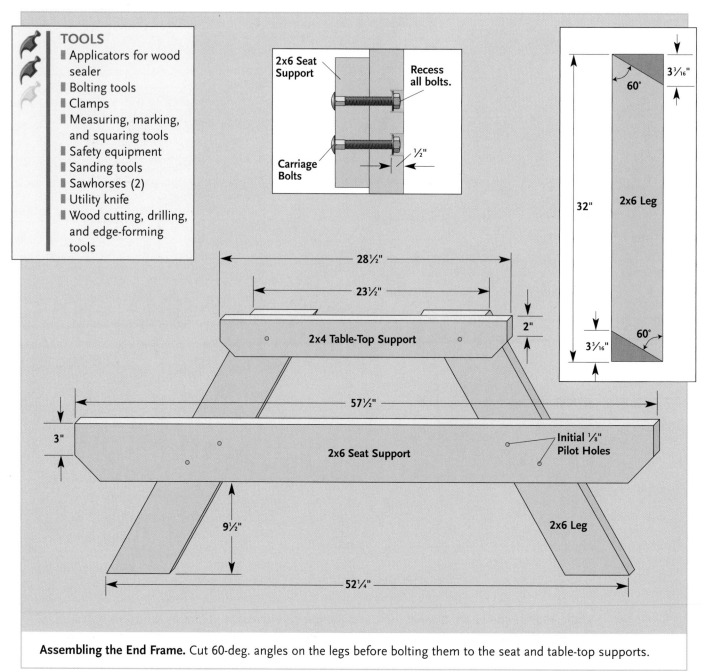

TOOLS
- Applicators for wood sealer
- Bolting tools
- Clamps
- Measuring, marking, and squaring tools
- Safety equipment
- Sanding tools
- Sawhorses (2)
- Utility knife
- Wood cutting, drilling, and edge-forming tools

2x6 Seat Support

Recess all bolts.

Carriage Bolts

½"

32"

2x6 Leg

60°

3³⁄₁₆"

60°

3³⁄₁₆"

28½"

23½"

2x4 Table-Top Support

2"

57½"

3"

2x6 Seat Support

Initial ⅛" Pilot Holes

9½"

2x6 Leg

52¼"

Assembling the End Frame. Cut 60-deg. angles on the legs before bolting them to the seat and table-top supports.

ASSEMBLING THE SEATS AND TOPS

The four seat boards and five table-top boards are each 48-inch 2x6s. Draw a squared line across each board 8¾ inches from each end. Then start two screws along each line about 1 inch inside the edge, without driving them through the seat board.

If working alone, hold up one of the end braces, and finish driving one screw through an outside seat board into the center of the support, flush with the end of the support. Next, attach the outside board to the other seat on the same end brace. Then attach both boards to the other end brace. This job is easier if you have a helper or two to hold up the end braces.

Using a framing square to ensure that the supports are perpendicular to the seat boards, drive each of the remaining screws. Next, attach the inside seat boards on both sides, being sure

lumber and materials order

LUMBER

Lumber	Quantity	Size
2x6s	1	12'
	6	8'
2x4	1	12'

HARDWARE AND MORE

Materials	Quantity	Size
Carriage bolts, nuts, and washers	12	⅜" x 3"
Deck screws	60	2½"
Finish		

CUTTING LIST

	Quantity	Size
Tabletop supports	2	2x4 28½"
Seat supports	2	2x6 57½"
Legs	4	2x6 32"
Tabletop and seat boards	9	2x6 48"
Center brace	1	2x4 27"
Diagonal braces	2	2x4 19¼"

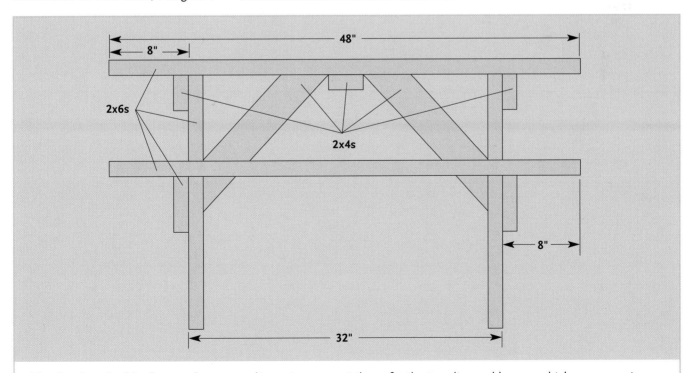

The drawings in this chapter show exact dimensions except those for the two diagonal braces, which are approximated. To determine exact brace dimensions, create cardboard templates after assembling all other components. For this, see the next page.

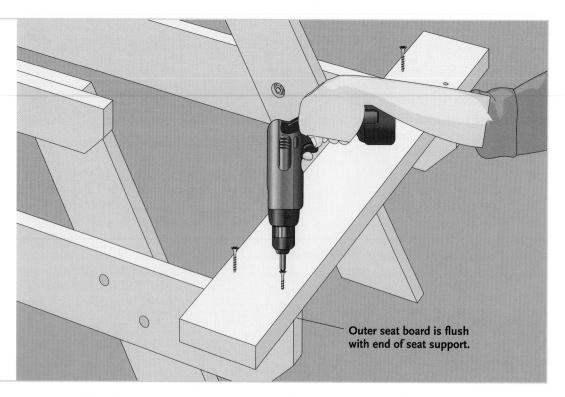

Postpone driving the second screw on each side until after you attach the second outside seat board and squaring the two boards, as shown at right.

Outer seat board is flush with end of seat support.

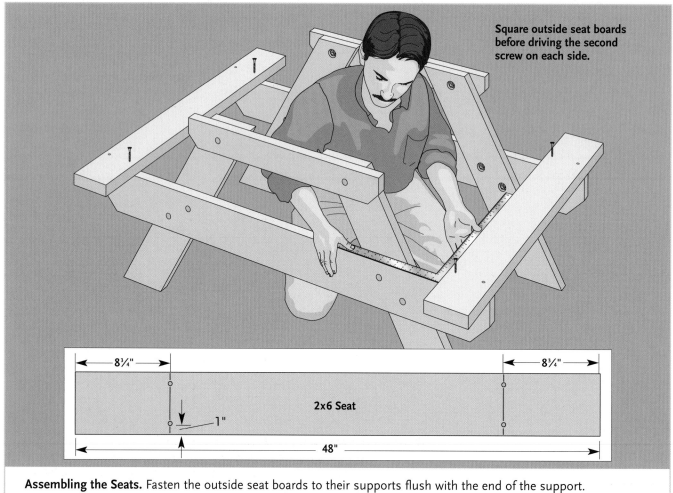

Square outside seat boards before driving the second screw on each side.

| ← 8¾" → | 2x6 Seat | ← 8¾" → |

1"

48"

Assembling the Seats. Fasten the outside seat boards to their supports flush with the end of the support.

to leave a ¼-inch gap between them and their outside board.

Position table top boards, keeping outside boards flush with ends of support boards. Keep gaps between boards ¼ inch. Screw the boards to the end braces.

ATTACHING THE BRACES

The 2x4 bracing on the table is composed of two diagonal braces and one center brace. The center brace is 27 inches long, its sharp end corners broken by a 45-degree bevel.

Note: the diagonal braces are cut at different angles on each end. Because your assembled dimensions may vary from ours at this point, the 20¾-inch length suggested for the diagonal braces should be regarded only as an approximation. To avoid wasting wood, first transfer your measurements and angles to a piece of cardboard; then cut the cardboard using a utility knife. Set the template in place on the table, and check the fit. Trim the template until the edges are flush with their mating surfaces. When you have found just the right length and angles for the cardboard template, trace its pattern onto the 2x4s.

Turn the table over, and screw the braces into place, driving screws through the diagonal braces at an angle into the seat support and tabletop. Be careful not to drive screws through the topside of the table itself or through the seat supports.

SMOOTHING AND FINISHING

Round-over cut edges, and smooth any rough edges using sandpaper. Wipe down the table using a damp cloth. Then apply a water-repellent finish or exterior stain.

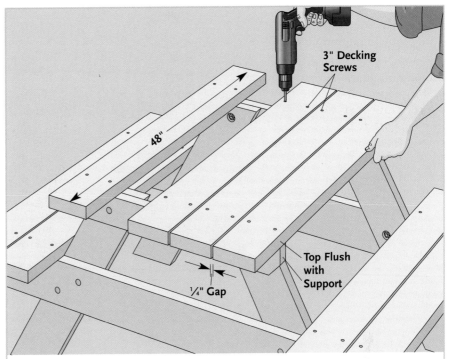

Assembling the Top. Install outside boards flush with ends of supports, using 3-in. decking screws or 8d galvanized nails. Maintain a ¼-in. gap.

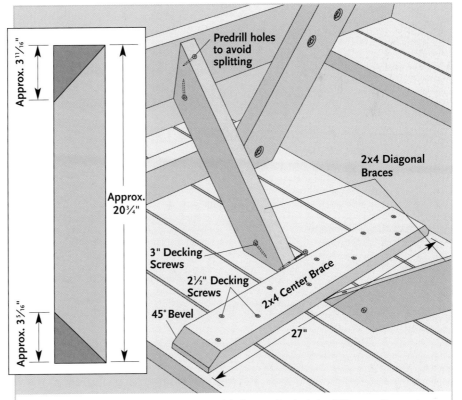

Attaching the Braces. If your assembly has only slightly different dimensions than prescribed, angles and lengths of your braces may need to be different from those shown. For best results, create test-fitted cardboard templates for each brace, and transfer their outlines to the 2x4 before cutting.

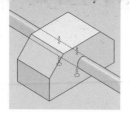

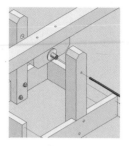

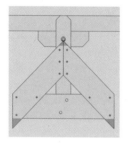

12 teeter-totter

Not long ago the teeter-totter, or seesaw, was as common on public playgrounds as swings and slides. Because of potentially hazardous misuse, teeter-totters are seen less often, and seldom on new playgrounds. The design shown here is for younger children, before they reach an age when daredevil antics become common. This Teeter-totter is small and relatively short so that a child on the high end is never at a dangerous height. It is also portable and easily moved, or removed, from the play area.

Before they are allowed to use the Teeter-totter, all children should be instructed in these basic rules:

■ Only two children are allowed on the Teeter-totter at a time.

■ Only children of comparable weights should pair up.

■ All other children should stay well away from the users.

BUILDING THE SEAT ASSEMBLY

Cut the seat assembly from 4x4s to the following lengths: one 9 feet, seven 12 inches, two 7 inches, and two 6 inches. If you use a table saw, radial arm saw, or power miter saw, you can make cuts in one pass. The smaller blade of a circular saw will require two careful passes, one in front and one in back. Also cut two 13½-inch lengths of 1-inch hardwood dowel for the handles.

1 Make the Seat Blocks and Bumpers. The four seat blocks are made exactly the same. Lay out and drill ⁷⁄₁₆-inch-diameter holes in each block, but wait until Step 5 to drill them. Miter the ends of the seat blocks and bumpers as shown.

2 Make the Handle Blocks. The two sets of handle blocks are identical. Lay out and drill the 1-inch-diameter dowel hole in the center of the upper block. Miter both ends of each block.

TOOLS
- Applicators for wood sealer
- Bolting tools
- Clamps
- Measuring, marking, and squaring tools
- Metal-cutting saw
- Mill file
- Safety equipment
- Sanding tools
- Sawhorses (2)
- Utility knife
- Wood cutting, drilling, and edge-forming tools

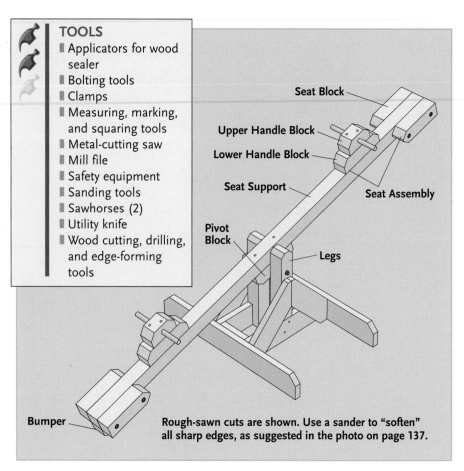

Rough-sawn cuts are shown. Use a sander to "soften" all sharp edges, as suggested in the photo on page 137.

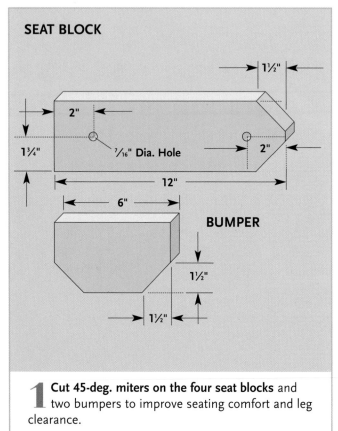

SEAT BLOCK

1½" · 2" · 1¾" · ⁷⁄₁₆" Dia. Hole · 2" · 12"

BUMPER

6" · 1½" · 1½"

1 Cut 45-deg. miters on the four seat blocks and two bumpers to improve seating comfort and leg clearance.

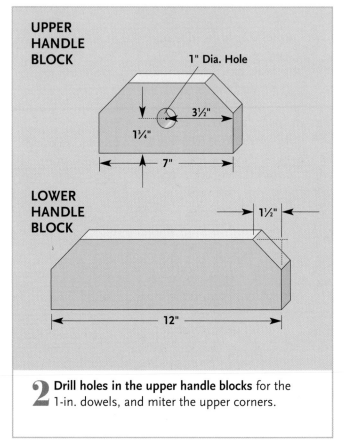

UPPER HANDLE BLOCK

1" Dia. Hole · 3½" · 1¾" · 7"

LOWER HANDLE BLOCK

1½" · 12"

2 Drill holes in the upper handle blocks for the 1-in. dowels, and miter the upper corners.

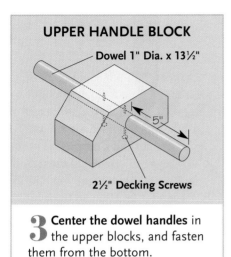

UPPER HANDLE BLOCK

Dowel 1" Dia. x 13½"

5"

2½" Decking Screws

3 **Center the dowel handles** in the upper blocks, and fasten them from the bottom.

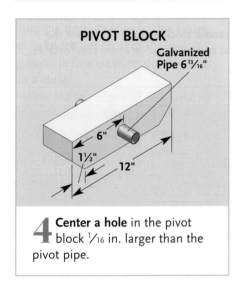

PIVOT BLOCK

Galvanized
Pipe 6¹³⁄₁₆"

6"

1½"

12"

4 **Center a hole** in the pivot block ¹⁄₁₆ in. larger than the pivot pipe.

3 **Attach the Handles.** Cut and insert the dowels into the holes on upper handle blocks. You may need to hammer the dowels lightly, centering them with a 5-inch exposure on each side. Then drive two 2½-inch decking screws through the bottom of the block into each dowel.

4 **Make the Pivot Block.** The pivot block is identical to the handle blocks except that it requires a larger hole. The 1⅛-inch-diameter hole shown here assumes that you are making the pivot with galvanized steel pipe that has a 1¹⁄₁₆-inch outside diameter. This is the typical outside diameter of ¾-inch galvanized pipe, but measure first. Be sure to drill the hole slightly larger than the pipe.

lumber and materials order

LUMBER

Lumber	Quantity	Size
4x4	2	12'
2x6	3	8'
Hardwood dowel	1	1" x 36"

HARDWARE AND MORE

Materials	Quantity	Size
Carriage bolts, nuts, and washers	8	⅜" x 10½"
	2	⅜" x 7"
	4	⅜" x 4"
Lag screws, washers	4	⅜" x 5½"
Threaded steel rod	1	⅜" x 13"
Locking nuts, washers	2	⅜"
Galvanized steel pipe	1	¾" x 8" (nominal)
Washers	2	3"
Deck screws	4	2½"
	44	3"
Finish		

CUTTING LIST

	Quantity	Size
Seat support	1	4x4 9"
Seat blocks	4	4x4 12"
Lower handle blocks	2	4x4 12"
Pivot block	1	4x4 12"
Upper handle blocks	2	4x4 7"
Bumpers	2	4x4 6"
Legs	2	4x4 23¼"
Lateral ground supports	2	2x6 43"
Leg supports	2	2x6 24"
Spacers	2	2x6 7¹³⁄₁₆"
Cross braces	4	2x6 22½"
Hardwood dowels	2	1" x 13½"

ASSEMBLE THE TEETER-TOTTER

The final steps involve attaching the legs to the seat assembly. With the addition of bracing and supports, the construction will be complete.

1 Join Legs to Seat Assembly. With a helper or two, stand the two legs upright. Raising one end of the seat assembly, move its pivot block into position between the legs, and then slide the pivot pipe through the legs and pivot block. Slip the ⅜ x 13-inch threaded rod through the pivot pipe so that it protrudes equally on both sides of the posts.

Slide washers over the threaded rod on each side. Then loosely fasten locknuts on each side (you may need two socket wrenches to tighten the locknuts). Attach the 2x6 spacers between the legs with 3-inch decking screws, as shown below.

Finish tightening the locknuts. Avoid overtightening, which would restrict the movement of the Teeter-totter. With a metal-cutting blade, cut off the protruding ends of the threaded rod. Then file off any sharp metal.

2 Add Bracing. Cross bracing on each side helps support the legs. Make four braces from 22½-inch 2x6s, cut with 45-degree miters as shown. Check each pair of braces for a proper fit; then trim off the sharp tips. Attach braces to the legs with 3-inch decking screws.

3 Attach Supports. To ensure that the Teeter-totter won't tip sideways, add two lateral ground supports of 43-inch 2x6s. Miter the top corners on each, and then fasten the supports to the legs with 3-inch decking screws.

Finishing Touches. Round-over all sharp edges and sand the entire Teeter-totter. Apply the finish of your choice. You may notice that the rocking motion is a bit stiff immediately after assembly. But with continued use, the stiffness vanishes. Overly tightened locknuts can also restrict the up and down motion.

HAND TOOLS OR POWER TOOLS

This project requires that you make a series of square cuts and drill several well-aligned holes in 4x4s. The work can be done with hand tools, but only if you work carefully. You'll get more accurate results using stationary power tools. Cutting will go best with a table-saw, radial arm saw, or power miter saw. As for drilling, we recommend a drill press or a drill guide.

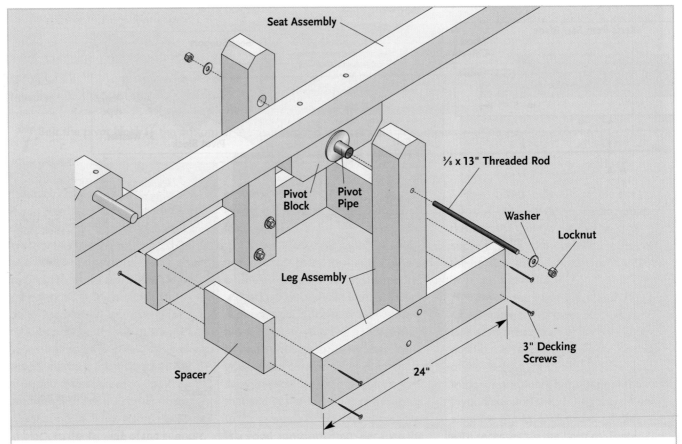

1 **To join the legs to the seat assembly,** insert the pivot rod on the assembly into the legs. Then secure the assembly with threaded rod and 2x6 spacers.

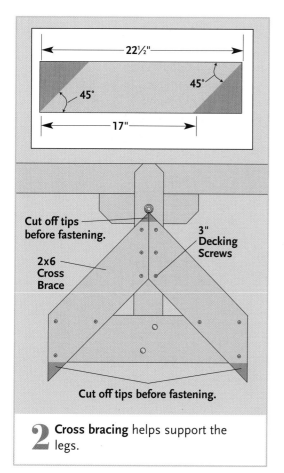

22½"

45°

45°

17"

Cut off tips
before fastening.

3"
Decking
Screws

2x6
Cross
Brace

Cut off tips before fastening.

2 **Cross bracing** helps support the legs.

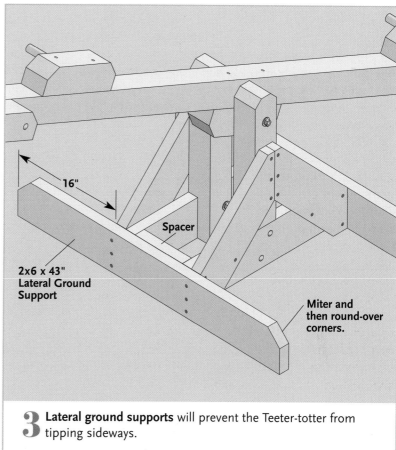

16"

Spacer

2x6 x 43"
Lateral Ground
Support

Miter and
then round-over
corners.

3 **Lateral ground supports** will prevent the Teeter-totter from tipping sideways.

If the threaded rod protrudes after you tighten the locknuts, saw it off with a metal-cutting blade and file the sharp edges smooth.

PART FOUR

For something a little different, consider adding one of the three projects in this section: a playhouse and two tree houses. They are more challenging to build than the play structure, but they will provide hours of fun for kids in a wide age group. And each adds a distinctive look to your yard.

Although it remains firmly anchored to the ground, the playhouse may be the most complicated of the three projects—think of building a house in miniature. But once finished, it will be a kid favorite. The two tree houses provide a chance to add a distinctive play area to your yard that makes it different from the other yards in the neighborhood.

ADVANCED PROJECTS

13 Victorian playhouse

This compact playhouse—just 60 square feet—is a wonderful destination for your kids, a place of their own where they can make up the rules (at least some of them!) and take responsibility for keeping it clean inside and out. By installing a full-sized door on one end, this building becomes a spacious storage shed for all those things that clog a garage, such as lawn mowers, garden hoses, and leaf blowers.

This playhouse features a Victorian design with a steep roof, multiple gables, and faux gingerbread trim. If you'd like something that matches the design of your own house, just modify these plans so the roof pitch, roofing material, trim, and color scheme match the main house. The following pages, of course, show how to build this specific playhouse. But the techniques discussed constitute a concise primer for building any small structure.

SITE PREPARATION

The easiest way to start this project is to establish the location of the 6 foundation blocks; level them in place; and start building the floor deck. But spending a little more time on this job will yield better results. By removing the sod, setting the blocks, and covering the ground between and around the blocks with crushed stone, you'll get a surface that will drain away ground water better, and at the same time reduce the number of weeds growing up against the building. Less water and weeds under the building means a drier building that will last much longer.

The best way to remove the sod, especially if you want to use it in some other place, is to use a sod cutter. These walk-behind machines are common rental items and cost about $50 a day, if you have access to a pickup truck or van. This machine slices under the grass and into the soil to create a mat that's about 2 inches thick x 16 inches wide. You can cut these strips to 2 feet lengths, roll them up, and keep them watered until you install them elsewhere. If you don't want to use the sod, then just till up the ground, rake out the plant matter, and roll the soil flat.

Install the foundation blocks so they are level and square. Then fill the tilled area with 2 or 3 inches of No. 2 crushed stone, and roll the surface smooth.

If you want to build this playhouse as part of a larger job that includes other projects such as a Central Tower, Monkey Bars, and a Swing Frame, then consider making the site excavation bigger so it extends under every structure. In this case, make the excavation deeper (at least 4 inches); install landscape fabric to inhibit future weed growth; and fill the area with one of the impact-reducing materials discussed on page 17.

Victorian playhouse

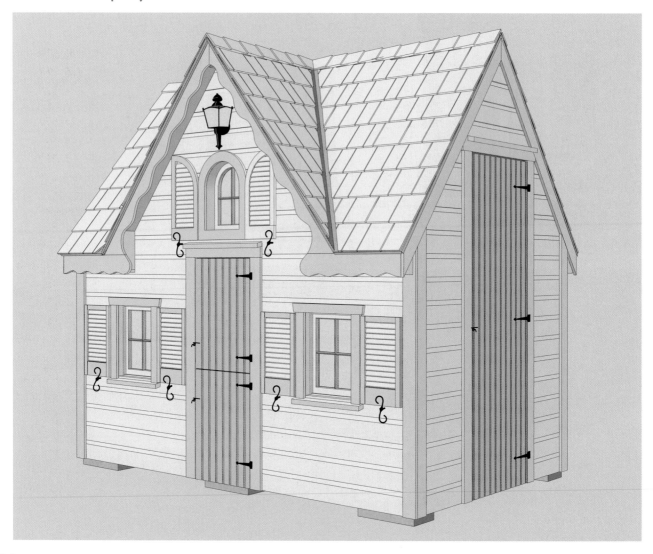

lumber, materials, and cutting list

LUMBER AND MATERIALS ORDER

Lumber	Quantity	Size
2x6s	5	12'
	6	10'
	2	8'
2x4s	27	12'
1x8s	1	12'
1x6s	6	8'
1x4s	15	8'
1x3s	4	8'
$\frac{5}{4}$ x4s	1	8'
1x6 tongue-and-groove boards	9	8'
Car siding	300 sq. ft.	1x6
$\frac{5}{8}$" PT plywood	2	4'x8' sheets
$\frac{1}{2}$" CDX plywood	7	4'x8' sheets

HARDWARE AND MORE

Materials	Quantity	Size
Concrete blocks	6	4" x 8" x 16"
Barn sash windows	2	16" x 20"
Arched top window	1	16" x 20"
Shutters	4	10" x 20"
Half-arch shutters	2	10" x 20" (custom)
Roofing felt	175 sq. ft.	30-lb.
Roofing	200 sq. ft.	Cedar shingles
Ridge cap	10'	Preformed cedar cap shingles
Roof edging	50'	Aluminum drip edge
Hinges	7	6" heavy-duty strap hinges
Latch	2	Thumb latches
Lamp	1	Exterior light fixture
Fasteners	14	2x6 joist hangers
	10 lbs.	16d galvanized nails
	10 lbs.	16d coated sinker nails
	10 lbs.	8d coated box nails, or
	10 lbs.	$1\frac{1}{2}$" galvanized deck screws
	20 lbs.	8d galvanized siding nails
	15 lbs.	$1\frac{1}{4}$" roofing nails
	5 lbs.	8d galvanized finish nails
	15 lbs.	6d galvanized cedar shingle nails

Primer and Paint

CUTTING LIST

	Quantity	Size
Rim joists	4	2x6 10'
Floor joists	9	2x6 66"
Floor plywood $\frac{5}{8}$"	2	4' x 6'
Floor plywood $\frac{5}{8}$"	2	2' x 3'
Sidewall plates	6	2x4 10'
Left end-wall plates	2	2x4 6'
Right end-wall plate	1	2x4 65"
Right end-wall plates	4	2x4 $21\frac{1}{2}$"
Right end-wall plates	2	2x4 $16\frac{1}{2}$"
Wall studs	24	2x4 48"
Right wall door studs	2	2x4 $80\frac{1}{4}$"
Windowsills and headers	4	2x4 $16\frac{1}{2}$"
Right wall door header	1	2x4 29"
Full rafters	13	2x6 $69\frac{1}{8}$"
Ridge board	1	2x8 10'
Short rafters	4	2x6 $60\frac{1}{2}$"
Dormer opening rafter	1	2x6 $27\frac{7}{8}$"
Collar ties	7	2x4 30"
Roof plywood $\frac{1}{2}$" CDX	3	4'x8' sheets (cut to fit)
Dormer ridge	1	2x6 40"
Short dormer rafter	2	2x6 $29\frac{7}{8}$"
Long dormer rafters	2	2x6 $55\frac{7}{16}$"
Dormer roof $\frac{1}{2}$" CDX plywood	2	$42\frac{1}{8}$" x $67\frac{3}{8}$" triangles
Back roof soffit board	1	1x6 10'
Back roof fascia board	1	1x8 10'
Dormer overhang supports	2	2x6 cut to fit
Front roof soffit boards	2	1x6 28"
Front roof fascia boards	2	1x6 $29\frac{3}{4}$"
Dormer rake boards	2	1x8 68"
Corner boards	4	1x4 cut to fit
Rake boards	4	1x4 cut to fit
Door trim	6	1x4 cut to fit
Window trim	6	1x3 cut to fit
T&G large door boards	6	1x6 $81\frac{1}{4}$"
T&G small door boards	5	1x6 $56\frac{1}{2}$"
Large door battens	3	1x6 $25\frac{3}{4}$"
Small door battens	4	1x4 $18\frac{5}{8}$"
Diagonal door battens	4	1x4 cut to fit

FOUNDATION

Once the site is prepared, drive stakes as shown, and pull a mason's string tight between the stakes so it forms a rectangle that's 6 feet wide x 10 feet long. Make sure the corners are square by checking them with a framing square or by comparing diagonal measurements from corner to corner. If both diagonals are the same length, the strings are square. Also make sure the strings are level and are located about 2 inches above where you want the top of the foundation blocks to be. Use a line level to make sure the strings are level. Once the blocks are installed, you can double-check for level by holding a 4-foot level on one edge of a 10-foot 2x4 and checking that all the blocks align.

After the strings are properly adjusted, place a concrete block at each corner, and remove or add soil underneath each until the block aligns with the string. Establish the exact distance between the top of the first block and the string; then use this dimension to

FOUNDATION AND FLOOR JOISTS

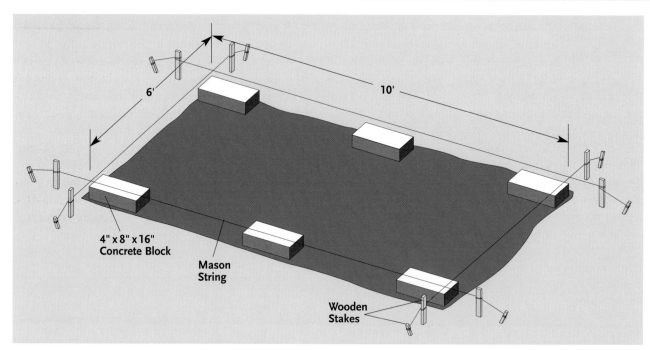

6'   10'

4" x 8" x 16"
Concrete Block

Mason
String

Wooden
Stakes

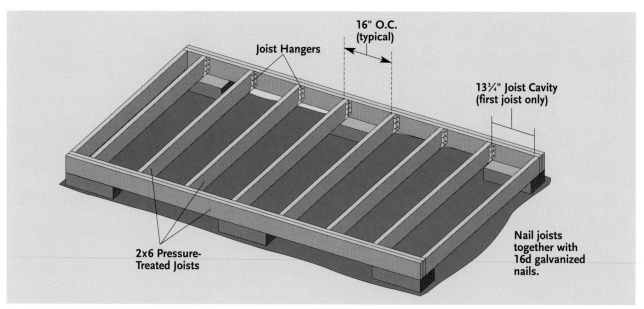

Joist Hangers

16" O.C.
(typical)

13¾" Joist Cavity
(first joist only)

2x6 Pressure-
Treated Joists

Nail joists
together with
16d galvanized
nails.

locate the other blocks. With the corner blocks installed, add the middle blocks on the long sides; then remove the strings and stakes.

DECK FRAMING

Begin the first floor deck framing by cutting all the joists to exact length, and laying out the rim joist on both long sides to match the joists spacing indicated in the drawing. Then install 2x6 galvanized joists hangers at the joist locations to carry the load between the foundation blocks. Place the two rim joists with the hangers on the foundation blocks. Slide the floor joists between, and nail them in place, through the outside of the rim joist, using 16d galvanized nails. Also nail the sides of the joist-hanger flanges into the sides of the joists using galvanized joist-hanger nails. Finish up the deck by nailing an extra rim joist to the long sides.

Note: The floor framing calls for pressure-treated lumber. This is usually the best choice when building outdoor projects because of its resistance to moisture and insect damage. But pressure-treated lumber does cost more and is much heavier, so it's harder to maneuver. If you live in an area where snow won't pile up against the building, then you can save money by using construction-grade lumber.

Deck Sheathing

The first floor deck is completed once the floor plywood is installed. Use ⅝-inch-thick pressure-treated plywood if you want the building to last as a storage shed after its days as a kid's playhouse. But as mentioned elsewhere, this material is expensive and heavy. So if you'd like to save some money and effort, use ⅝-inch CDX plywood, instead.

The joists are laid out so a full-width (48 inches) plywood panel will cover the end joist and extend to the middle of the fourth joist from the end. The second sheet fits against the first one and extends to the middle of the seventh joist from the end. Cover the last two joists spaces with the pieces that you cut off from the other two sheets. Typically, floor plywood is installed so the length of the panel is perpendicular to the direction of the joists. But because this deck is designed so all the plywood joints fall over the top of a joist—and are therefore completely supported—placing the sheets as shown here is the most efficient use of material.

The standard nails used for floor plywood are 8d box nails. But 1½-inches-long galvanized deck screws are better. They cost a little more and take more time to install. But they do a better job of holding the plywood to the joists. Drive the screws around the perimeter of each panel and into each floor joist every 5 to 6 inches Use a ⅜-inch electric drill for this job, or a 12- or 14-amp cordless drill. The corded tool is more powerful, but the cordless models are more convenient.

FLOOR DECKING

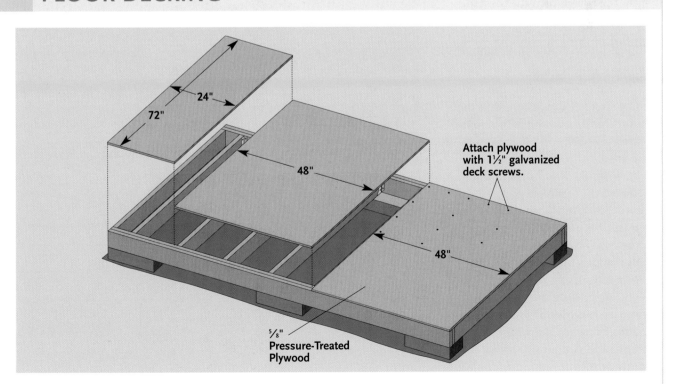

24"
72"
48"
48"

Attach plywood with 1½" galvanized deck screws.

⅝" **Pressure-Treated Plywood**

WALL FRAMING

These wall framing components are made of 2x4 construction lumber, often referred to as SPF (spruce/pine/fir) lumber. While this material is very strong and durable, it's not always straight. Because of this, it's important to examine each piece of lumber that you use. If a board is extremely crooked, anything more than $1/8$ inch of distortion per two feet of length, set this board aside, and use it only for small blocks or return it to the supplier for credit. Lumberyards will usually take back crooked lumber. But if you are buying your material in a home center, select straight boards before you buy them.

Start each wall by cutting the plates and studs to length. Then lay out the wall plates so the studs will fall on 16-inch centers. Mark the bottom and top layout plates at the same time to ensure that the studs will be installed plumb. Then separate the plates, and slide the wall studs between them. Work on top of the floor deck so you'll have a wide, flat surface to keep everything aligned. Hold each stud next to its layout; mark and nail the plate into the end of the stud with two 16d sinker nails. Finish each wall, and set aside until all the walls are built.

Note that one end wall has an opening for a full-sized door, while the front wall has an opening for a smaller kid-sized door and two windows. These are the only wall openings in this building. But if you want to add windows to the other end wall or the back wall, just create openings for them that match the size of the windows on the front wall.

The windows used on this project are recycled windows salvaged from another building. While this is a good way to get inexpensive windows, it can take some searching around, depending on where you live. A strategy that will probably work better for most people is to use the barn sashes specified here.

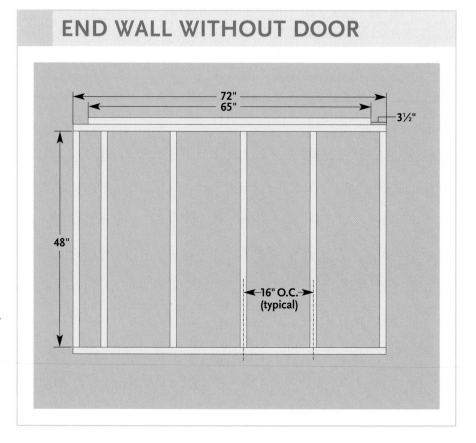

END WALL WITH DOOR

29"   1½"
Stud notched for gable rafter
39.4°
20"
16½"
3½"
72¹³⁄₁₆"
80¼"
72½"
21½"
Notched stud side view

END WALL WITHOUT DOOR

72"
65"
3½"
48"
16" O.C. (typical)

These inexpensive wood windows are just simple sashes—no jambs, casings, or flashing are included—designed to fill wall openings in barn walls. They come in various sizes and have a simple, traditional design. Not all home centers carry them. But lumberyards usually do, either in stock or as an ordered item. No matter what windows you chose, have them on site before

you begin the project. By doing this, you can take exact measurements of the window, and frame your wall openings to match them, which is easier than estimating the opening and then making the window fit.

The fussiest part of building these walls is cutting the studs on the side of the full door to size. Unlike the other end wall that is built to the same height

as the front and back wall, this wall is built to reach the roof rafters so there will be enough headroom to operate the door. Because of this, the door studs extend from the bottom plate to the back of the gable rafters above. These studs need a 1½-inch-wide notch cut in their front edge so their outside edge will sit flush with the outside edge of the rafters.

FRONT AND BACK WALLS

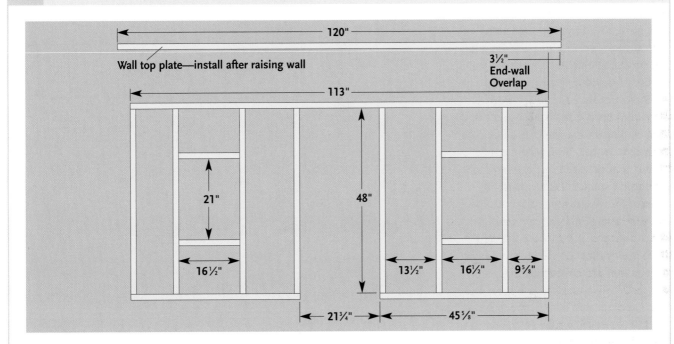

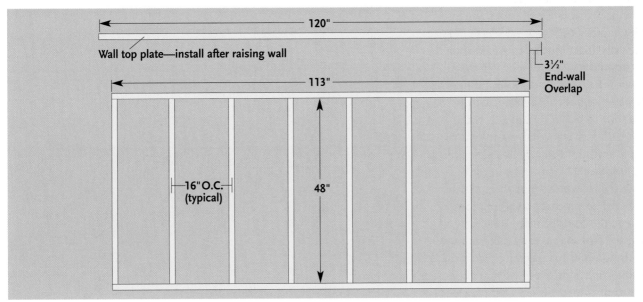

RAISING WALLS

While none of these walls is very heavy, you will need help moving, lifting, and supporting them. You can start with any wall that's convenient. But if the site doesn't dictate a preference, start with the back wall, followed by the end walls, and the front wall. First lift the wall onto the deck, and raise it so it's flush with the back edge of the floor. Locate the bottom plate so it's $3\frac{1}{2}$ inches in from both ends of the floor deck to allow for the end walls. Once the wall is in the right spot, nail it to the deck so it's flush with the side of the back rim joist.

Nail a diagonal brace that goes from the top of the middle wall stud down to a wood block nailed to the plywood floor. Plumb the wall with a 2- or 4-foot level, and nail the brace to the block. At this point the back wall will be a little wobbly, so don't lean on it or run into it with one of the other walls. Next, lift one of the end walls into place and have a helper hold it. Nail the bottom plate to the floor so it's flush with the deck on the side and ends. Then nail the corner studs of the back and end walls together. Do the same with the other end wall. Once the two corners are nailed together, you can remove the center brace.

Finish up by lifting the front wall into place and nailing it to the deck and the end walls. Install the top plates that reinforce all the walls, as shown in the drawing. Be sure to drive nails through the plates above each stud location.

Installing Siding

Before you start installing the siding, nail a diagonal brace on the inside of all the walls. Nail one end of a 10-foot 2x4 to the side of the top plates, and push the other end against the side of the bottom plate. Plumb each wall and hold it in this plumb position while you nail the bottom end of the brace to the bottom plate. With the braces nailed, all the walls should be plumb and square.

ASSEMBLING WALLS

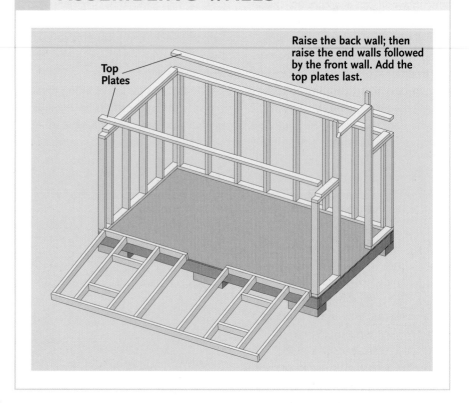

Top Plates

Raise the back wall; then raise the end walls followed by the front wall. Add the top plates last.

INSTALLING SIDING

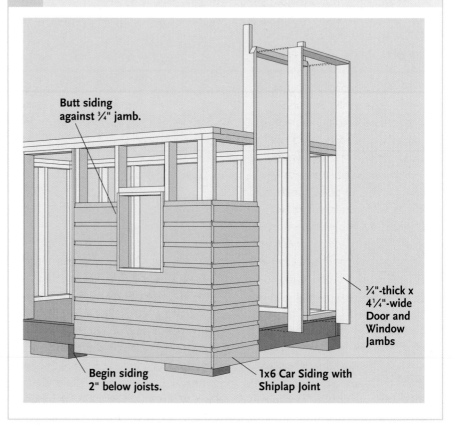

Butt siding against ¾" jamb.

Begin siding 2" below joists.

1x6 Car Siding with Shiplap Joint

¾"-thick x 4¼"-wide Door and Window Jambs

Start installing the siding at the bottom of the wall, making cuts as necessary to fit around the windows and doors. The car siding used here has a shiplap joint on the top and bottom edges, so it's easy to install. Once the walls are covered with siding, install the window and door jamb boards as shown.

ROOF FRAMING

On this playhouse all the rafters are identical except for the four that fall under the front dormer. These are missing the rafter tail that extends beyond the front wall.

The drawing below right shows profiles of the roof rafters. Carefully mark and cut one full rafter to use as a pattern. Then trace its outline on the rest of the 2x6 rafter stock. On the rafters that fall under the dormer, omit the tails. Just extend the vertical bird's mouth cut to the top of the rafter. Cut the ridge board and collar ties.

The roof ridge on this building is located about 8 feet above the floor, so you'll need scaffolding to be able to fit and install the parts. One easy way to build a scaffold is to place a couple of 2x8s or 2x10s on a pair of sawhorses in the middle of the floor. Temporarily screw these planks to the sawhorses.

Start the roof assembly by nailing a pair of front and rear gable rafters to their respective wall plates. Have a helper hold these in place above the scaffolding while you and another helper install the gable rafters at the other end of the building. Have the second helper hold them in place while you lift up the ridge board, and squeeze it between the four rafter ends.

With the helpers holding the parts together, join the rafters to the ridge by driving 16d sinker nails through the ridge into the ends of the rafters. Once both ends are nailed together, install a temporary diagonal brace from one end of the ridge to a stake driven into the

ground about 10 feet away from the end of the building. Make sure that the end of the ridge board is plumb with the outside edge of the end wall before nailing the brace to the stake.

Install the rest of the rafters in the same way: nail their bird's mouth cuts to the wall plates first, then to the ridge. When you reach the rafter space that falls above the dormer opening,

note that this rafter is cut short to fit between a rafter header and the ridge. This creates an opening in the roof for the light that comes from the dormer window. Nail the rafter header between its neighboring rafters, and cut and install the short rafter above it. Once all the rafters are in place, install the collar ties as shown, and add the gable studs above the far end wall.

RAFTERS

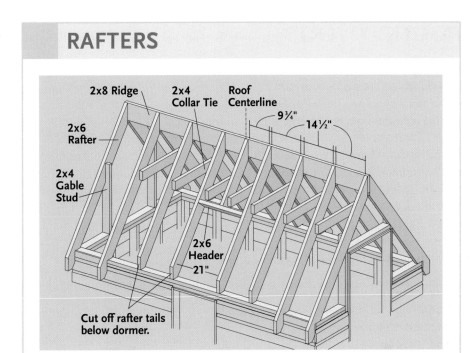

RAFTER LAYOUT

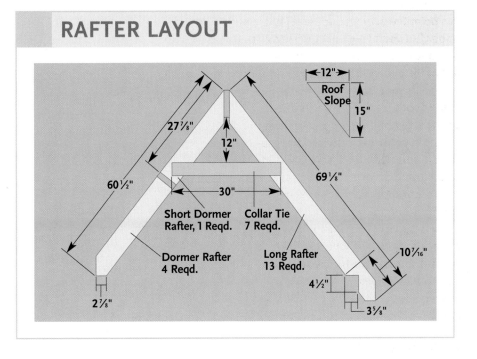

ROOF PLYWOOD

Installing the roof plywood is a straightforward job on the back of the roof. Because this side has no dormer, you just run the plywood from end to end, making sure that any joints fall directly over a rafter. Before installing any plywood, nail the soffit and fascia boards to the back side rafter tails. Place the plywood sheets on top of the rafters so their bottom edges extend just $\frac{1}{8}$ inch beyond the edge of the fascia board. Nail each sheet to every rafter that it covers using 6d nails spaced about 6 inches apart.

On the front roof, the plywood does not cover the area below the dormer. If it did, the light that comes through the dormer window wouldn't reach inside.

To cut the bottom sheets, use the detail drawing below as a guide. Then lift the panels up, and nail them to the rafters so their bottom edge extends past the rafter tails about $\frac{3}{4}$ inch. To make sure that the plywood panels are straight, snap a chalk line across the rafters, from one end of the building to the other, that's $47\frac{1}{8}$ inches above the end of the rafter tails.

front roof deck

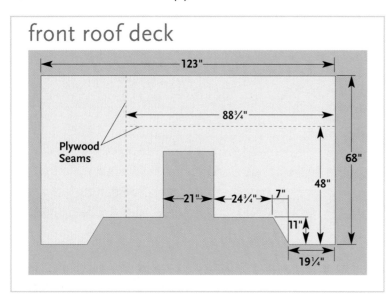

dormer rafters & ridge

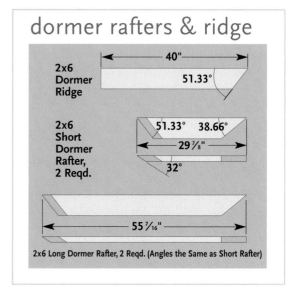

DORMER FRAMING

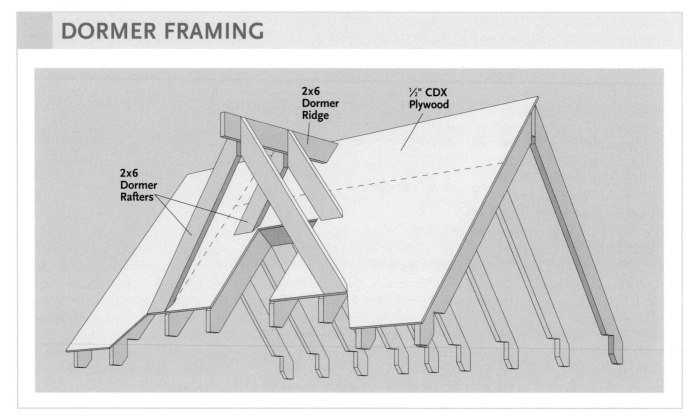

DORMER SIDING AND ROOF

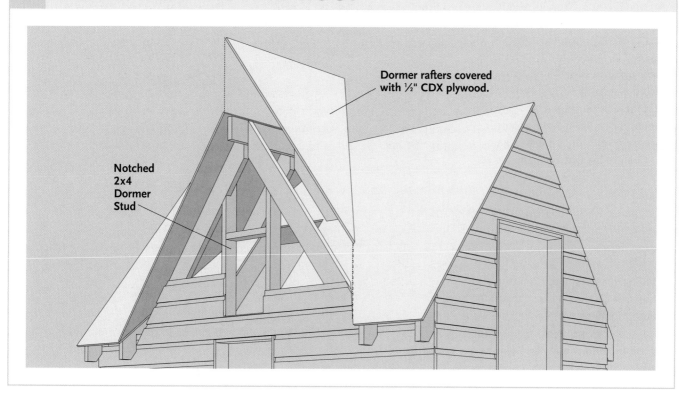

Dormer rafters covered with ½" CDX plywood.

Notched 2x4 Dormer Stud

Dormer Framing

Once all the plywood is nailed to the roof, start framing the dormer that sits on the front roof. Cut the ridge and rafter boards to the size and shape shown in the drawings, opposite top right. Then nail these components to the roof, starting with the longer rafters, followed by the ridge, followed by the smaller rafters. You'll need help for this job, too. One helper holding each long rafter in place should do the trick. Before you nail the rafters to the ridge, slide the ridge in place and make sure it's level. Note that the ridge board extends past the front rafters to support that overhang that will be attached to the dormer gable once the siding is in place.

Dormer Roof Plywood

Both sides of the dormer roof are covered with the same-size piece of ½-inch plywood. Use the drawing, right, as a guide. But before you cut the plywood, double check to make sure that

the size shown will fit your roof. Slight variations in the building process can alter finished dimensions. So take accurate measurements on the roof, and check them against our plans. If there's a discrepancy, chose the field measurements, not the plans. Once you're satisfied, cut these panels, and nail them to the dormer rafters. The plywood should extend beyond the gable rafter far enough to cover the overhang that will come later.

Dormer Siding

With the dormer framed and the plywood installed, cut the gable studs that define the gable window opening. Nail them between the wall plate and the dormer rafters. These studs need a notch cut in the front edge to allow the rafters to sit flush against the studs.

Before you install the siding on the front of the dormer, make sure you have your dormer window on site. This playhouse features a salvaged window with an arched top. If you want to make

the job a little easier, use a barn sash for this window, like the ones you used on the front wall. Once the window rough opening is established, cut the siding boards to size, and install them on the dormer gable.

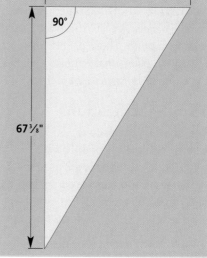

dormer plywood pattern

42 ⅛"

90°

67 ⅜"

ROOF OVERHANGS

The main roof and the dormer roof both have overhangs. The main overhangs are built around the rafter tails, while the dormer overhang is constructed against the gable and runs between the dormer ridge board and the adjacent rafters on the main roof.

Typically you would build these overhangs before the plywood is installed on the roof. But because this project required that the roof plywood be installed before the dormer is constructed, it made more sense to finish the plywood work before doing the trim on the front of the building.

Begin by installing the 2x6 trim support boards on the dormer gable. Take measurements off the building to establish the exact width of these boards. Then rip them to width, and hold the boards in place so you can scribe the angle where they meet the ridge board and rafters. Cut these angles; then nail both boards to the dormer gable. Next, install the soffit boards under the main roof rafters, and nail the trim support blocks between the soffit boards and the rafter support boards, shown top.

After the overhang boards are in place, install the roofing to protect the building from the weather. This playhouse features cedar shingles applied over 30-pound felt. Be sure to install a drip edge along the rakes and eaves, and cover the roof ridge with premade cap shingle panels, available from your cedar roofing supplier. These panels cost more than plain, unassembled shingles, but using them saves a lot of time.

Trim Specifications

The drawing, opposite top left, shows all the components of the playhouse trim. No. 2 pine boards are used for everything, including the corner boards and rakes. These are applied over the surface of the siding, not abutting it. The same is true of the window and door casings.

ROOF OVERHANG

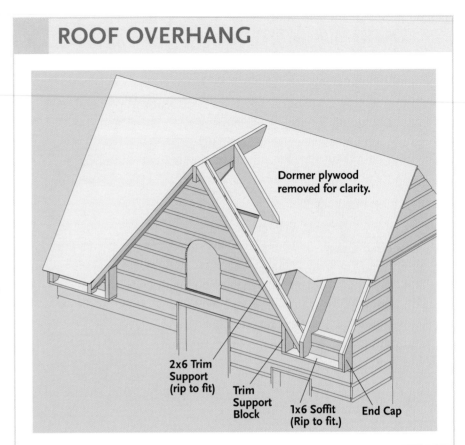

Dormer plywood removed for clarity.

2x6 Trim Support (rip to fit)

Trim Support Block

1x6 Soffit (Rip to fit.)

End Cap

ROOFING

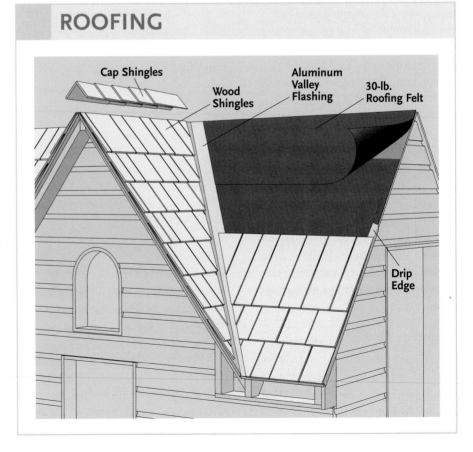

Cap Shingles

Wood Shingles

Aluminum Valley Flashing

30-lb. Roofing Felt

Drip Edge

WINDOWS AND TRIM

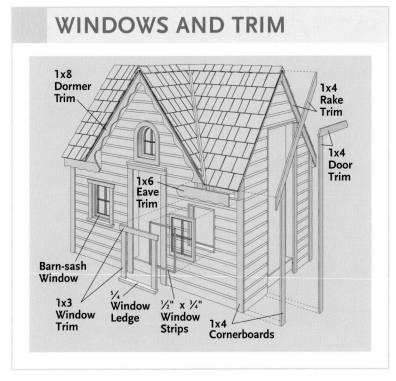

1x8 Dormer Trim

1x4 Rake Trim

1x4 Door Trim

1x6 Eave Trim

Barn-sash Window

1x3 Window Trim

⁵⁄₄ Window Ledge

½" x ¾" Window Strips

1x4 Cornerboards

doors

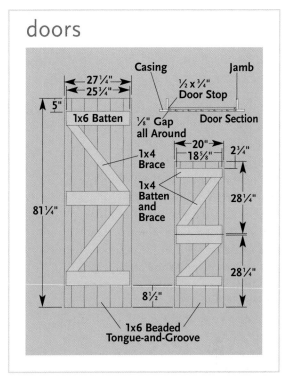

27¼"
25¾"

5"

1x6 Batten

Casing

Jamb

½ x ¾ Door Stop

Door Section

⅛" Gap all Around

81¼"

1x4 Brace

1x4 Batten and Brace

20"
18⅝"

2¾"

28¼"

28¼"

8½"

1x6 Beaded Tongue-and-Groove

fascia and rake patterns

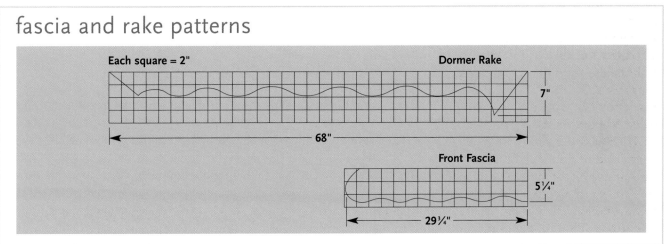

Each square = 2"

Dormer Rake

7"

68"

Front Fascia

5¼"

29¾"

The roof fascia boards and dormer trim on the front feature a rudimentary gingerbread design. Use the patterns shown above to mark these boards. Then cut the shapes using a jig saw, and smooth the cuts using sandpaper and wood rasps, if necessary. Keep in mind that all the trim boards should be primed on all six sides before they are installed. This is essential to the long-term life of any paint job. Even if you plan to stain this building, be sure to apply stain or a clear sealer to all of the surfaces.

The windows can be hinged, if desired, so they open from inside. Just install two ¾ x 2½ inches hinges to each. Once the sashes are installed, cut and nail the window stop strips to the jams, and cover these strips with the casing boards. Once the windows are installed, attach the shutters to the sides of the window with screws. Or, use the traditional shutter hinges and shutter dogs shown.

Finish up the construction by building the front Dutch door and the side door according the plans provided here.

Hang them in place using strap hinges and simple thumb latches available at home centers and hardware stores. Prime and paint the building with one coat of acrylic primer, followed by two top coats of 100 percent acrylic paint to create a long-lasting finish.

Install an inexpensive lantern light above the front entry door, if you want to duplicate the treatment we show here. While it might be nice to have this light work, running power from the main house to make it work may not be worth the trouble.

159

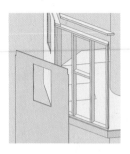

14 tree-house fort

Few things capture a kid's imagination like a traditional tree house. Built off of the ground, it offers great views of the neighborhood, catches the cool breezes that skip over the backyard below, and even delivers a little welcome freedom from parental control. If the structure has enough room (like this one does), the kids can stretch out and read books, sit against a wall and play cards, or just lean on a windowsill and watch the clouds go by.

As much fun as a tree house can be, it's also a little dangerous because it's up in the air. Because of this, it makes sense to build an enclosed structure rather than an open platform. Once you have the floor platform built, you can construct the wall modules either on the ground or up on the deck. Just keep in mind that working above the ground can be dangerous. So, get some help, use sturdy ladders, and don't rush things.

SITE SELECTION

Finding an appropriate tree is the starting point for any tree house project. A good rule of thumb is to choose one that is at least 16 inches in diameter and has a clear (free of branches) trunk from the ground to the top of where the tree house roof will fall. Small branches of an inch or two aren't a problem. Just cut them off using a chainsaw or a bow saw. But larger branches that support a lot of smaller branches and leaves are another issue. By cutting them off you will be reducing the shade the tree provides and you might not want to do that. Keep in mind that the bigger the tree, the less

it will sway in a stiff wind, which makes for a better, longer-lasting tree house. Also make a study of the tree's health. If the trunk looks sound and the leaves are green, then you probably have a good candidate. But if you aren't sure about a given tree, it's a good idea to have an arborist look at it. Arborists are usually listed in the Yellow Pages, and are a great source of tree information.

Consider the ground around the tree, too. Steeply sloping sites don't provide a stable surface for an access ladder. They can also make the construction harder. And don't even consider building the structure near overhead power or phone lines. Don't select a tree too

close to the house, especially if it's situated so an enterprising child could climb from the tree house onto a branch then onto the house roof. It's hard to imagine anything good coming from such a journey.

And finally, check with your local building department before you do any work. If you live in a rural area, it is not likely that any code requirements exist. But in suburban areas, the chances of you needing a building permit go up. They probably don't want to regulate how you build a temporary structure such as a tree house, but they may well want to establish it's location—how close to your property line, the street, and your neighbor's house.

tree-house fort

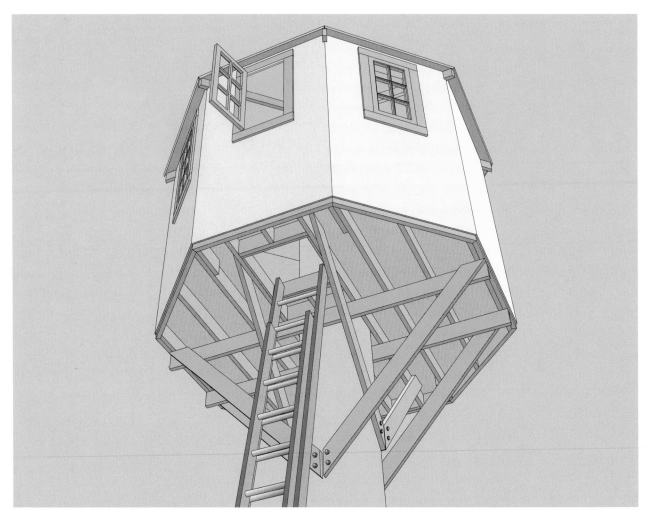

lumber, materials, and cutting list

LUMBER AND MATERIALS ORDER

Lumber	Quantity	Size
2x6s	9	10'
	17	12'
	3	14'
	3	16'
2x4s	15	16'
1x4s	5	16'
⅝" T&G plywood	3	4'x8' sheets
½" AC plywood	8	4'x8' sheets
½" CDX plywood	4	4'x8' sheets

HARDWARE AND MORE

Materials	Quantity	Size
Barn sash windows	7	16" x 30"
Roofing felt	170 sq.ft.	30 lb.
Roof edging	35 ft.	Aluminum drip edge
Fiberglass shingles	200 sq.ft.	3 tab
Fasteners	20 lbs.	16d galvanized nails
	15 lbs.	2½" galvanized deck screws
	24 lbs.	½" x6" galvanized lag screws
	30 lbs.	1½" galvanized deck screws
	10 lbs.	1¼" galvanized deck screws
	20 lbs.	1¼" galvanized roofing nails
	5 lbs.	8d galvanized finishing nails
Hardware	14 pair	¾" x 3" galvanized butt hinge
	1 pair	6" galvanized T-hinge
Coatings	1 gal.	Plastic roof cement
	1 gal.	Exterior latex primer
	1 gal.	Exterior latex paint

CUTTING LIST

	Quantity	Size
Lower beam braces	4	2x6 80½"
Lower beams	2	2x6 114⅞"
Upper beam braces	4	2x6 71"
Upper beams	2	2x6 111⅞"
Cross blocks	5	2x6 23⅜"
Long floor joists	2	2x6 111⅞"
Middle floor joists	2	2x6 82⁹⁄₁₆"
Short floor joists	2	2x6 49⁵⁄₁₆"
Filler joist	1	2x6 41⅜"
Hatch blocking (outside)	1	2x6 6⁷⁄₁₆"
Hatch blocking (inside)	1	2x6 10"
Rim joists	8	2x6 47⁹⁄₁₆"
⅝" T&G plywood	3	4'x8' sheets
Wall plates	16	2x4 47⁹⁄₁₆"
Top wall plates	8	2x4 49⅝"
End wall studs	16	2x6 67½"
Middle wall studs	16	2x4 67½"
Window framing	16	2x4 15"
½" AC plywood	8	48" x 77⅞" sheets
Rafters	8	2x6 63⁵⁄₁₆"
Short rafter blocks	8	2x6 9"
Middle rafter blocks	8	2x6 21⁵⁄₁₆"
Middle rafter blocks	8	2x6 33⅝"
Long rafter blocks	8	2x4 46¹⁵⁄₁₆"
½" CDX plywood	8	48" x 52" sheets
½" CDX plywood	8	10" x 16¼" pieces
Window trim	14	1x4 30" No. 2 pine
Window trim	14	1x4 23" No. 2 pine
Hatch trim	2	1x6 23⅜" No. 2 pine
Hatch trim	2	1x6 21⅞" No. 2 pine

LOWER BEAMS AND BRACING

The tree-house floor is supported by two sets of beams, which are supported by diagonal braces attached to the tree. The length of the beams is based on the tree house we built here. If you are building a larger (or smaller) one, adjust the dimensions to match yours. Begin fabricating these beams by cutting the parts to the size and shape shown below, and joining them with 2 ½ inch galvanized deck screws.

Establish the proper height for the top edge of a lower unit, and mark the tree with a piece of sidewalk chalk. Then nail the beam to the trunk just below this line using 16d galvanized common nails. Have a helper hold a level on the top of the beam, and adjust it so it is level. Then tack-nail the bottom of the braces to the trunk. Check for level again, and if it's okay, drill screw clearance holes through the beam and braces into the tree for ½-inch-diameter x 6-inch lag screws. Push the lag screws into these holes, and tighten the screws using a socket or open-end wrench.

Use the same procedure to attach the second lower beam to the other side of the tree. When you check this beam for level from end to end, make sure you also check that it's level with the first beam.

Once both beams are in place and level, attach some temporary braces to maintain level during the construction process. To do this, just measure the distance from the end of each beam to the ground, then cut a 2x4 to the same length. Place one end on the ground, the other next to a beam, and nail the brace to the beam. Keep in mind that the beams on both sides should be approximately parallel at this point. If they are slightly skewed, don't be concerned. The proper spacing can be established later, once the upper beams are in place.

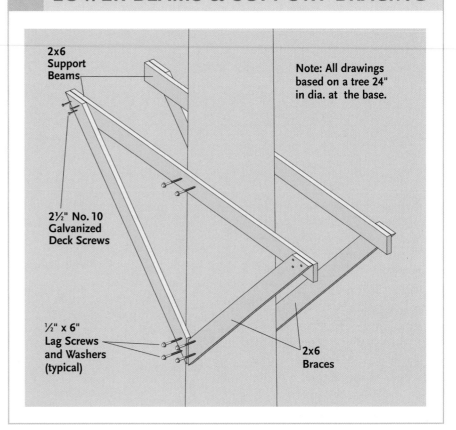

LOWER BEAMS & SUPPORT BRACING

2x6 Support Beams

Note: All drawings based on a tree 24" in dia. at the base.

2½" No. 10 Galvanized Deck Screws

½" x 6" Lag Screws and Washers (typical)

2x6 Braces

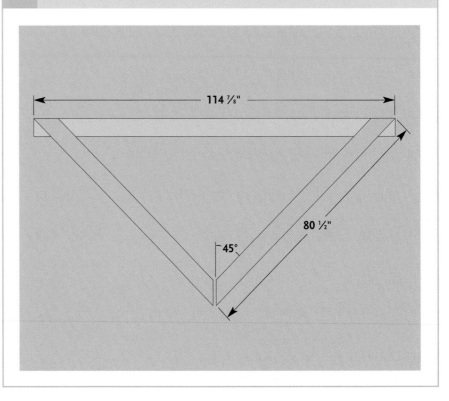

LOWER BEAM & BRACE SPECS

114 ⅞"

80 ½"

45°

UPPER BEAMS AND BRACING

The upper beams and their braces are similar to the lower ones, but they are assembled differently. Instead of joining all the parts together so they are rigid triangles before lifting them in place, the braces in the upper units are joined to the beams with just one screw per end. This allows you to move the braces out of the way when you lower the upper beams onto the lower beams. Once the beams are in place, the braces can be pivoted together and attached to the tree.

Start building the upper beam box by joining the beams together with the short cross blocks on one side of the trunk only. Keep in mind that the locations of the cross blocks next to the tree depend on the diameter of the tree you are using. (The beams must be located so that the center of the trunk is at the center point of the beams. And the cross blocks should fall next to the trunk so the lag screws can be driven directly into the trunk.) Attach each brace with one screw; then lift the assembly onto the top of the lower beams. You'll need some help sliding the beams around the tree trunk while you keep the upper beam braces from getting tangled in the lower beams assembly.

When the upper beam assembly is in place, cut the remaining cross blocks (that fall on the other side of the trunk) to size, and screw them in place between the beams. Then rotate the upper beams as necessary until they're square with the lower beam, and toenail the beams together so they stay square. Check the top edge of the upper beams for level; then bolt the beams and cross blocks to the tree. Attach the support braces to the tree as shown in the drawing, top. To keep the beams level during construction, cut and install temporary braces from the end of the beams to the ground as you did with the lower beams. At this point you'll have eight braces extending to the ground. Keep them in place until the floor plywood is attached.

UPPER BEAMS AND BRACES

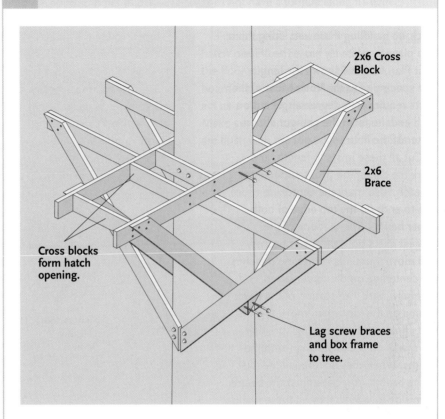

2x6 Cross Block

2x6 Brace

Cross blocks form hatch opening.

Lag screw braces and box frame to tree.

UPPER BEAM & BRACING SPECS

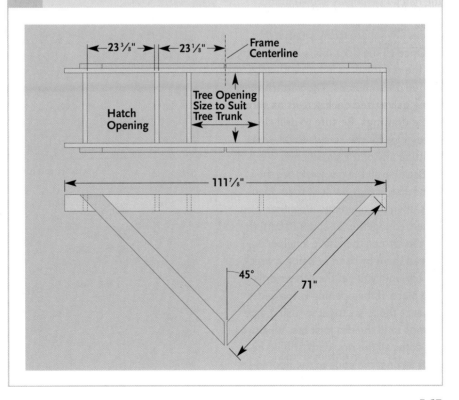

23 3/8"

23 1/8"

Frame Centerline

Hatch Opening

Tree Opening Size to Suit Tree Trunk

111 7/8"

45°

71"

WALL BUILDING

These walls are designed so that each is an identical module. Because of this, you can build the eight individual frames on the ground, and carry them up and nail them in place, one after another. Or, you can cut the boards on the ground and assemble the walls on the deck. Before you start building, make sure that the tree house deck is the same dimension on all eight sides.

Start this job by laying out the location of all the walls on top of the floor plywood. At each corner, measure 3½ inches in from the outside of the rim joists, and make a mark. Then connect these marks by snapping a chalk line between them. When you are done, you should have a line around the perimeter of the deck that's 3 ½ inches (the width of a 2x4 wall plate) in from the outside. Once these lines are established, draw a line from where they intersect at each corner to the outside corner formed by the rim joists. Then carefully measure each side to make sure they are all the same length.

If they are each within ⅛ inch of the same measurement, then you can build all the walls the same size. If their lengths differ by ¼ inch or more, you'll have to build each wall individually to fit its side. Assuming the sides are equal, cut all the parts for the walls at the same time using the drawing opposite as a guide. Make the cuts using a circular saw, and try to minimize the waste. If you have access to a power miter box or a chop saw, use one of these. They make cutting 2x4 and 2x6 stock much easier. And, both can cut angles up to 45 degrees.

Note: The end studs on each wall module are angled to form the octagon shape of the tree house. To fill the space properly, these studs must be cut from 2x6s instead of 2x4s. Do this job using a circular saw with a rip guide attached or a small portable table saw. After each wall is built, carry it up to the

deck, and have a helper hold it in place while you nail the bottom plate into the deck. With the helper holding up the first wall, retrieve the second wall, and nail it to the deck and to the end of the first wall. Have the helper hold both walls together while you get the next one. Install each section like this, until all the walls are in place. Then cut and install all the top plates to the walls so that everything is joined firmly together.

On larger walls, like those used to build a house, the next step is to brace the walls so they are straight and plumb. But because these walls are only about 4 feet long and not quite 6 feet high, no braces are required. It is, however, a good idea to take a few minutes and check the outside of each corner for plumb. If the walls are within ⅛ inch of plumb on a 4-foot level, then everything is fine. If they are farther out, then consider pulling the nails that hold the corners together, and forcing the joint in or out until it's plumb. When you are satisfied, nail the walls together again.

WALL ASSEMBLY

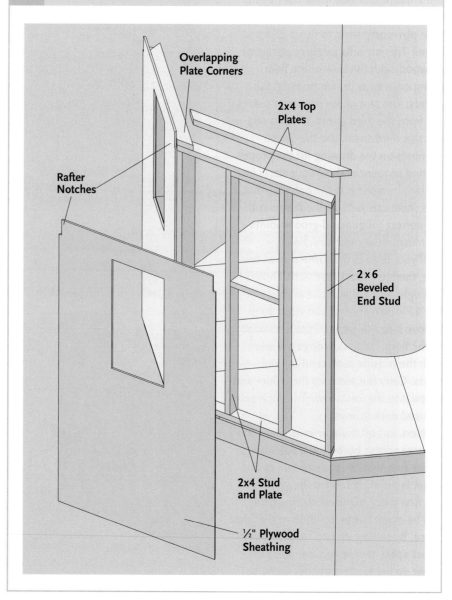

Overlapping Plate Corners

2x4 Top Plates

Rafter Notches

2 x 6 Beveled End Stud

2x4 Stud and Plate

½" Plywood Sheathing

INSTALLING THE WALL PLYWOOD

The ½-inch-thick plywood that functions as the sheathing and siding for this building has an AC rating. This means that one side (the A) has a high-quality surface with no cracks or knotholes in the top veneer. This is placed on the outside of the wall. The other side is graded C, which means that surface faults are allowed. The C side is placed on the inside of the wall. Make sure to stipulate that you want exterior-grade plywood because it features water-resistant glue to hold the laminations together. This type of plywood still needs a protective coating, in this case primer and paint. But it won't be damaged by the weather for a couple of weeks during the construction process.

Take careful measurements of the width of each wall. If they are all the same, then you can cut all the siding panels the same size. If they're not, then custom-cut each panel to fit it's wall. The drawing below gives the dimensions of the standard piece. **Note:** The designated width is 48 inches, the size of a typical sheet of plywood, and that both long edges need a 22 ½-degree bevel cut from bottom to top. This allows the siding panels to fit flush against each other at the corners.

Once the panels are cut, lift each into place against the wall framing and attach with 1¼-inch galvanized deck screws.

caution

ROOF FRAMING

The roof for this tree house features traditional rafter construction, but it doesn't have a typical ridge board. Instead, the tree trunk functions as the ridge; because the trunk is an irregular

WALL FRAMING DETAILS

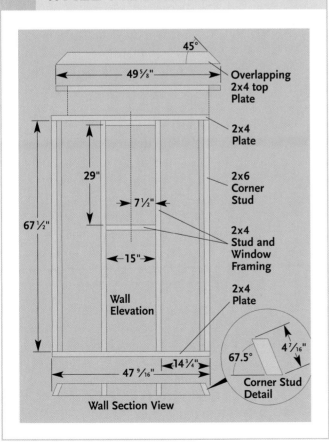

SIDING PANEL DETAILS

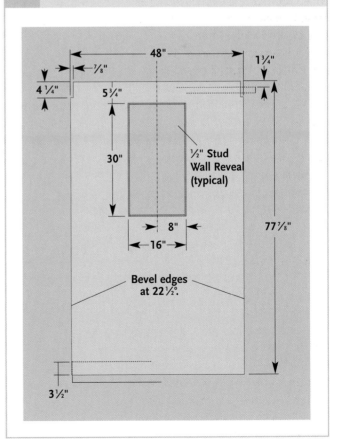

shape, each rafter needs to be custom cut to fit its spot.

Begin this job by creating a rafter pattern. The drawing, opposite top, shows the size rafter we used, but this may not work on your tree. The best approach is to create your own rafter pattern, using the rafter-positioning jig shown. Just place the jig on the floor and against the tree; then measure the distance from the tree at the bottom of the jig notch to the outside of the wall. Transfer this dimension to a 2x6 and mark the bird's-mouth cut for the wall plate. Also, mark a 6/12 slope on both ends using a framing square. Carefully cut this pattern using a circular saw;

then place it in the rafter jig's notch. If it fits tightly against the tree and the top of the wall plate, you have created a good pattern. Use this and the jig to check the other rafter positions, adding or subtracting length as necessary to get the best fit.

Once all the rafters are cut, toenail them on both sides of the bird's mouth into the wall plate below. Then tack-nail the top of each rafter to the tree trunk at its approximate position. Leave the head of this nail sticking up at least ½ inch so it will be easy to pull later. Then cut the rafter blocking to size and shape, and install it between each pair of rafters. If any rafter has to

move slightly for the blocking, pull the tack-nail and move the rafter. When all the blocking is installed, drive all the tack-nails so they're flush with the top edge of the rafters.

Next, cut the ½-inch-thick plywood panels to size and shape for the roof sheathing. Use construction grade exterior plywood, not AC panels, for this job. (They are less expensive and do a good job in places that won't show when the building is done.) Attach this sheathing with 1 ½-inch galvanized deck screws. Then cover the entire roof with 30-pound roofing felt, and install aluminum drip edge along the bottom edge. Finish up the roofing by in-

ROOF ASSEMBLY

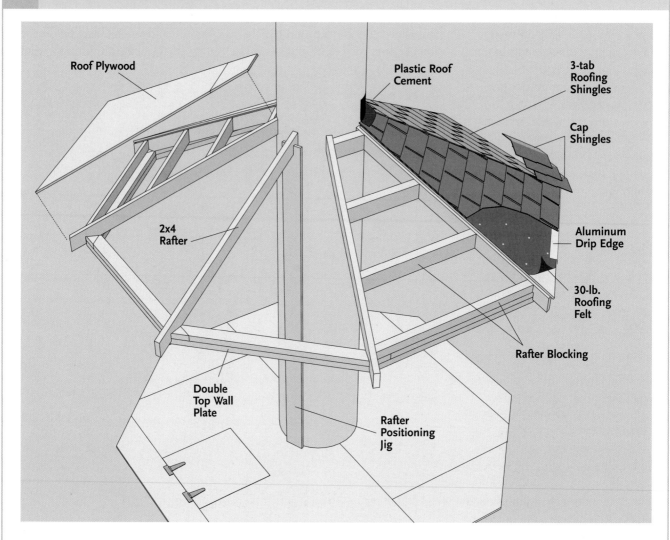

Roof Plywood

Plastic Roof Cement

3-tab Roofing Shingles

Cap Shingles

2x4 Rafter

Aluminum Drip Edge

30-lb. Roofing Felt

Rafter Blocking

Double Top Wall Plate

Rafter Positioning Jig

stalling 3-tab fiberglass shingles on the flat sections and single-tab fiberglass cap shingles where the roof sections meet. Seal the shingles to the tree with plenty of plastic roof cement. Over time, leaks are bound to open up. Rainwater will usually follow creases in the bark down to the ground. If you have a major leak, just apply more plastic cement.

INSTALLING THE WINDOWS

The windows used on this tree house are inexpensive 16 x 30-inch barn sash that are mounted on the exterior trim with common butt hinges. These sash are common stock items at lumber-yards and some home centers. Even if the size you want isn't available, it can usually be ordered. For the windows to work properly, the trim boards must be installed carefully so they create a square opening with a uniform 1/8-inch space around the perimeter of the window.

To ensure the trim is installed properly, measure the sash, then add 1/4 inch in height and width, and mark the siding plywood to indicate the inside edge of the trim boards. Then cut the boards to size, and tack-nail them (using the marks as a guide) to the siding with galvanized 8d finishing nails. Check the opening for square, and drive the nails flush with the surface of the boards. Mount the two butt hinges to the edge of the sash, and hold it in place to mark the hinge screw holes on the edge of the left trim board. Remove the sash; bore screw pilot holes at the marks; then lift the sash into the opening again, and attach the hinge with its screws. Check the window for proper operation; then mount a magnetic catch on the inside of the sash and the side of the window opening. This catch will keep the windows closed when desired.

ROOFING DETAILS

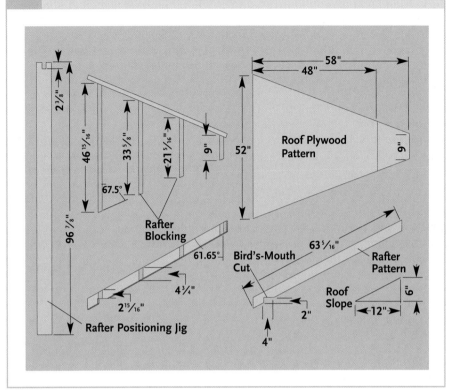

WINDOW DETAILS

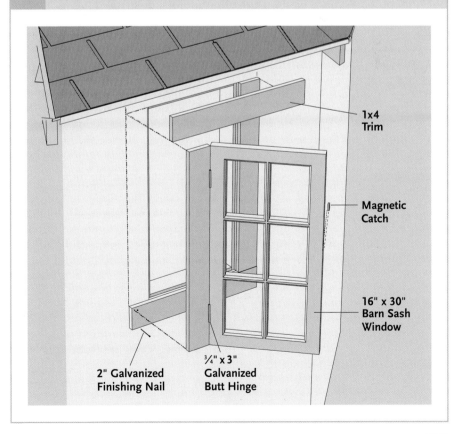

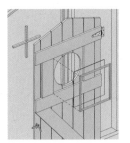

15 boat-style tree house

This clever playhouse and deck are designed to look like a boat floating through the trees. From the prominent prow in the front, to the rope railings along the sides, to the wheelhouse at the back, this structure makes the most of its nautical theme. And while it's not exactly a tree house—the trees don't support the structure—it does have a tree-house feel. At one end, the deck is elevated off the ground. And, from prow to stern, three trees poke through the floor. It may not be a tree house, but it certainly is a house in the trees.

Eye-catching looks are not the only good feature of this project. It also has a dual-use design. The enclosed section has almost 100 square feet of living space that's a welcome haven on cool, rainy days.

lumber, materials, and cutting list

LUMBER AND MATERIALS ORDER

Lumber	Quantity	Size
2x6s	13	14'
2x8s	44	14'
2x10s	1	8'
2x12s	5	16'
1x6 siding	420 sq.ft.	(cut to suit)
1x6s	11	8'
1x8s	6	14'
$\frac{1}{2}$" CDX plywood	6	4x8' sheets
$\frac{3}{4}$" quarter-round molding	4	8'
$1\frac{1}{2}$"-dia. lodge poles	60'	(cut to suit)
$1\frac{1}{2}$"-dia. hemp rope	50'	(cut to suit)

HARDWARE AND MORE

	Quantity	Size
Concrete blocks	2	4x8 x 16"
$\frac{1}{8}$" window acrylic sheet	6	$22\frac{1}{2}$" x $22\frac{1}{2}$"
$\frac{1}{8}$" door acrylic sheet	1	16" x 16"
30-lb. roofing felt	120 sq. ft.	Cut to suit
Alum. eave drip edge	2	$145\frac{1}{2}$"
Alum. gable drip edge	2	52"
3-tab fiberglass shingles	120 sq. ft.	
Fasteners	20 lb.	16d galvanized nails
	10 lb.	3" galvanized deck screws
	52	$\frac{1}{2}$" x 8" galvanized bolts and washers
	28	2x8 galvanized joist hangers
	25 lb.	$3\frac{1}{2}$" galvanized deck screws
	15 lb.	$2\frac{1}{2}$" galvanized siding nails
	15 lb.	1" galvanized roofing nails
	2 lb.	16d galvanized casing nails
	4	$\frac{1}{2}$" x 6" galvanized lag screws
Hardware	2	7" galvanized strap hinges
	1	Galvanized door latch
	5	Galvanized tread angles
Coatings	2 gal.	Wood-colored stain
	1 qt.	Green-colored stain

CUTTING LIST

	Quantity	Size
Support posts 4"-dia. P.T.	4	Length to suit
Long center beam	1	2x8 162"
Short center beam	1	2x8 67"
Long center beam	1	2x8 $146\frac{5}{16}$"
Short center beam	1	2x8 $82\frac{13}{16}$"
Support posts 4"-dia. P.T.	6	Length to suit
Outside rim joists P.T.	2	2x8 $134\frac{1}{2}$"
Inside rim joists P.T.	2	2x8 $138\frac{1}{2}$"
Outside-prow rim joists P.T.	2	2x8 $104\frac{5}{16}$"
Inside-prow rim joists P.T.	2	2x8 97"
Railing posts 4"-dia. P.T.	19	41"
Railing post 4"-dia. P.T. (nailed to side of building)	2	$32\frac{1}{4}$"
End joist P.T.	1	2x8 149"
Deck joists P.T.	10	2x8 135"
Prow joist P.T.	1	2x8 106"
Prow joist P.T.	1	2x8 74"
Prow joist P.T.	1	2x8 42"
Prow joist	1	2x8 10"
Wall studs	33	2x4 74"
Sidewall bottom plates P.T.	2	2x4 144"
End-wall bottom plate P.T.	1	2x4 89"
End-wall bottom plates P.T.	2	2x4 $26\frac{1}{2}$"
Sidewall top plates	2	2x4 144"
End-wall top plate	1	2x4 89"
End-wall top plates	2	2x4 25"
Window framing	12	2x4 $22\frac{1}{2}$"
Door studs	2	2x4 $89\frac{1}{2}$"
Door header	1	2x4 36"
Rough head jambs	2	2x4 $19\frac{1}{2}$"
Rafters	20	2x6 $51\frac{1}{4}$"
Ridge board	1	2x6 144"
Collar ties	8	2x4 42"
End-wall ridge support	1	2x4 15"
End-wall ridge support	1	2x4 $10\frac{1}{4}$"
Gable stud	2	2x4 $10\frac{7}{8}$"
Car siding 1x6	300 sq.ft.	Cut to suit
$\frac{3}{4}$" quarter round molding	4	77"
Gable trim	4	1x8 $54\frac{3}{8}$"
Gable eave	2	1x8 $145\frac{1}{2}$"
$\frac{1}{2}$" CDX plywood	6 sheets	48" x 52"
Prow board P.T.	1	2x8 $52\frac{1}{4}$"
Car siding for railing 1x6	120 sq.ft.	Cut to suit
$1\frac{1}{2}$"-dia, lodge pole trim	60 ft.	Cut to suit
$1\frac{1}{2}$"-dia. hemp rope	50 ft.	Cut to suit
2x12 window rings	36	24"

cutting list, cont'd

CUTTING LIST

	Quantity	Size
½" x ¾" retaining strip	12	22½"
½" x ¾" retaining strip	12	21½"
Door-jamb trim	2	1x6 70¼"
Door-jamb trim	2	1x6 19½"
¾" sq. door stop	2	18"
¾" sq. door stop	2	69½"
Door boards Pine	7	1x6 80" (cut to suit)
Door battens	3	1x6 34¼"
Door battens	1	1x6 16"
Diagonal door batten	1	1x6 45¾"
½" sq. door window strips	2	15"
½" sq. door window strips	2	16"
¾" sq. door mullion strips	2	7"

Note: P.T. stands for pressure-treated stock

SITE SELECTION

Selecting a site for a structure such as this involves several considerations. The first is the slope of the ground. The greater the slope is, the more dramatic the feel will be when someone is sitting on the deck. Unfortunately, the greater the slope, the harder the deck is to build. A site that drops more than 4 feet in 12 feet probably should be avoided.

The second consideration is the number of trees you want to incorporate into the design. In this case, three trees seemed like enough to create the right feel without making the construction too difficult. But with some careful planning, you don't have to incorporate any trees in the structure at all. Just locate the deck so that it falls between two or three trees that have large branches. These will overhang the structure just like trees that are designed to come up through the floor.

The third major consideration is how much time you want to spend on this project. If you are an experienced do-it-yourselfer, you should be able to finish this job in a couple of weeks if you have a little help holding some of the heavier pieces. But if you are new to carpentry work, plan on the job taking at least twice as long.

If the time is a big stumbling block for you, consider building just the deck or the playhouse. The drawings here show everything you need to build both, except for a simple foundation for the playhouse. For help building that, review the drawings on page 150 of the Victorian Playhouse story.

If you don't have a sloping backyard, you can still build our boat house by just elevating the entire deck at least three feet off the ground. This may not be as dramatic as what we show here. But when you combine this imaginative design with a great amenity like mature trees, you'll still be creating a very attractive place for your kids and their friends.

Because this structure combines a deck and a small building, you should contact your local building department to find out if you need a permit.

LUMBER SELECTION

Any horizontal wood structure that's exposed to the weather, such as this deck, should be built with rot-resistant lumber. Cedar and redwood are well known weather-resistant species. But they're also expensive and can be hard to find. Pressure-treated southern yellow pine is practically the default product these days.

Pressure-treated lumber is notorious for being heavy and crooked. You may need help carrying some of the longer boards. Discuss with your supplier (beforehand) the company's policy concerning returned wood. Some faults are to be expected. But avoid boards that have more than a ½ inch crown, cup, or warp within 10 feet of length.

boat-style tree house

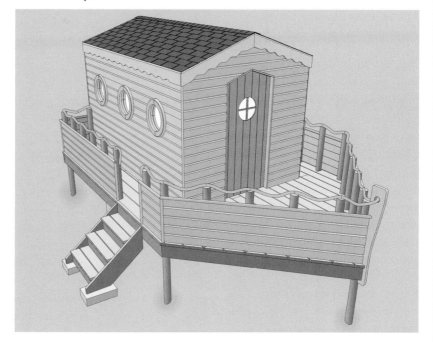

CENTER SUPPORT BEAM

The floor joists that form the deck structure are supported by posts on the perimeter and by a center beam that runs down the middle. This beam is made of two 2x8s that are joined with construction adhesive and galvanized 16d nails. The easiest way to build this beam is to assemble it in place, after the posts have been installed.

To install the posts, first establish the location of the four postholes, using the drawing right as a guide. Then dig the holes using a posthole digger or a rented power auger. The depth of each hole should be 4 inches below the frost line in your area. If you don't know how deep this is, check with your building department. Once the holes are dug, pour 4 inches of No. 2 crushed stone into the bottom of each.

Next, lower a pressure-treated post into each hole. On this job, we specified 4-inch diameter fence-rail stock. If this material isn't available in your area, then just use ground-contact 4x4s. The length of these posts will vary depending on the change in elevation between your holes. Just remember that these posts sit under the center beam, and this beam is under the joists. So if you know where you want the finished height of the deck to be, subtract 16 inches from this (1½ inches for the decking boards, 7¼ inches for the floor joists, and 7¼ inches for the beam) to determine the finished height of the posts. The post at the front of the deck extends much higher because it supports the front corner of the deck railing and the ornamental prow.

Once the posts are in place, brace them so they are plumb in both directions; then fill the hole around each with No. 2 crushed stone. Compact the stone with the end of a 2x4 as you pour it into the hole. Nail a double 2x8 joist hanger onto the side of the prowpost

CENTER SUPPORT BEAM AND POSTS

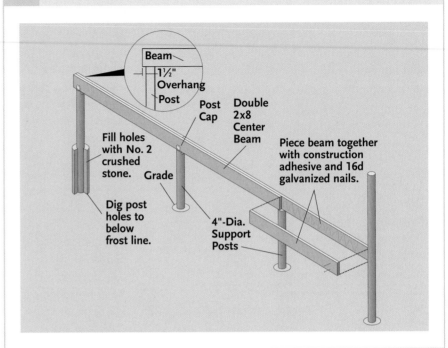

Beam
1½"
Overhang
Post
Post Cap
Double 2x8 Center Beam
Piece beam together with construction adhesive and 16d galvanized nails.
Fill holes with No. 2 crushed stone.
Grade
Dig post holes to below frost line.
4"-Dia. Support Posts

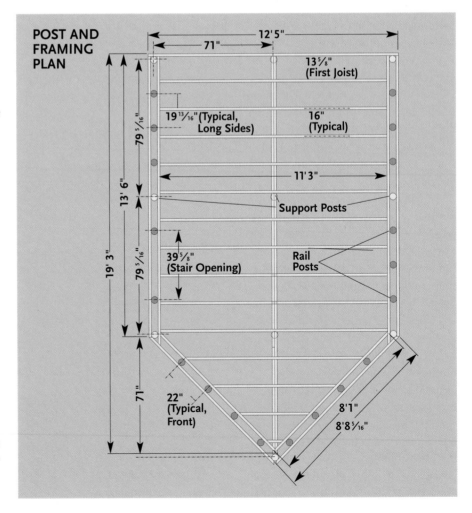

POST AND FRAMING PLAN

12' 5"
71"
13⅝" (First Joist)
19¹³⁄₁₆"(Typical, Long Sides)
16" (Typical)
11' 3"
Support Posts
39⅝" (Stair Opening)
Rail Posts
79⁵⁄₁₆"
13' 6"
79⁵⁄₁₆"
19' 3"
71"
22" (Typical, Front)
8'1"
8'8⁵⁄₁₆"

and 2x8 post caps on top of the other posts. Then build the center beam in place, using the drawing as a guide. Use plenty of construction adhesive and nails (in pairs, about 9–12 inches apart) for the strongest beam. Finish by nailing the post caps to the sides of the beams.

PERIMETER POSTS AND DECK JOISTS

In addition to the prow post, there are six perimeter support posts that are installed in the ground the same way that the center-beam posts were installed. But there is one big difference: all of these perimeter posts extend from the ground to the top of the deck railing.

When all these posts are installed, cut the inside rim joists to length, and check them for fit against the perimeter posts. Then lay out the floor joist position of these rim joists as shown in the drawing. Attach a joist hanger at each mark; then lift the rim joists into place, and nail them to the inside of the posts.

Next, tack-nail the outside rim joists to the outside of the posts so the top edge of each board is level with the top edge of the inside rim joists. Then cut the 4-inch diameter rail posts to a length of 41 inches, and start installing them between the inner and outer rim joists. Use $\frac{1}{2}$ x 8-inch galvanized hex-head bolts with nuts and washers for this job. Drill the clearance hole through both rim joists and the post. When the bolts are tightened in place, they will sandwich all three components together, which will strengthen the floor and the railing at the same time.

Once all the railing posts are installed, cut the floor joists to length, and slide them between the hangers and over the center support beam. Frame around the trees as required to provide support for the decking boards that come later. Toenail the joists into the top of the center beam, and attach their ends to the joist hangers with galvanized joist-hanger nails.

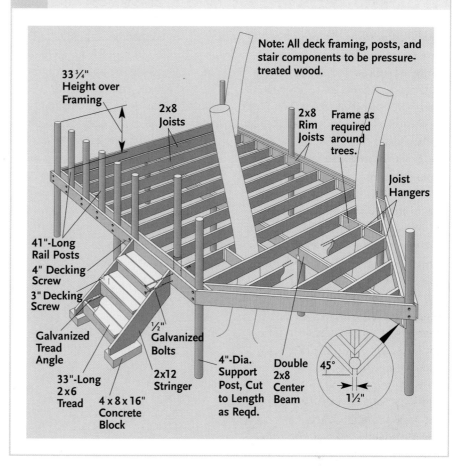

DECK AND STEP CONSTRUCTION

Note: All deck framing, posts, and stair components to be pressure-treated wood.

33¾" Height over Framing

2x8 Joists

2x8 Rim Joists

Frame as required around trees.

Joist Hangers

41"-Long Rail Posts

4" Decking Screw

3" Decking Screw

Galvanized Tread Angle

33"-Long 2x6 Tread

4 x 8 x 16" Concrete Block

½" Galvanized Bolts

2x12 Stringer

4"-Dia. Support Post, Cut to Length as Reqd.

Double 2x8 Center Beam

45°

1½"

STEPS

The steps that provide outside access to the deck are built with standard pressure-treated construction lumber. The sizes are shown in the drawing, right. You can make these steps using traditional dado and groove joints cut in the sides of the support stringers. But using galvanized tread angles makes the job much easier. Just lay out the stringers, and nail a tread angle under each tread location. Cut the treads to size, and nail through the angles to the underside of the treads. Join the risers to the treads with 4-inch galvanized deck screws. Drive the screws through the outside of the stringers into the ends of the risers and treads. Finish up by screwing the step assembly to the side of the deck rim joist.

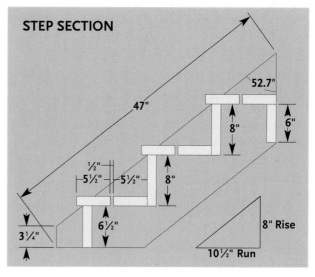

STEP SECTION

52.7°

47"

8"

6"

½"

5½"

5½"

8"

3¼"

6½"

8" Rise

10½" Run

INSTALLING THE DECK BOARDS

The deck boards on this project are pressure-treated 2x8s. These are substantial boards and make for a very strong deck. A good substitute material is 5/4x6 pressure-treated decking. These boards are lighter, easier to handle, and less expensive than 2x8s, but they still deliver a solid deck. No matter which pressure-treated stock you chose, keep in mind that excessively distorted boards are difficult and time-consuming to install. And even if you do work them into place, when they dry, they can split, cup, or twist so much that

you'll have to replace them. The better approach is to cut twisted boards into smaller lengths that are straighter, or simply set the bad boards aside and return them to the supplier for a credit.

Start installing the boards at one side of the deck. Push the board against the inside of the posts, and mark where all of the posts fall; then outline the post holes using the drawing as a guide. Remove the board and make the cuts using a jigsaw. Push the board against the posts again, check for proper fit, and adjust any of the cuts if necessary before screwing it to the joists. Use two 3-inch galvanized deck screws per joist, located so they hit the

rim joists below. Cut and install the edging board on the outside.

Continue installing the rest of the deck boards, maintaining a uniform 1/2-inch space between them. (Scrap pieces of 1/2-inch-thick plywood make good spacers.) Attach the boards with two 3-inch galvanized deck screws per joist, spaced about 1 inch in from both edges. Make sure that every seam in the deck boards falls over the middle of a joist, and be sure to drill screw clearance holes in both boards to prevent splitting from the screws. If you have trees coming through your deck, cut the deck boards so there's at least a 1-inch space between the boards and the trunk.

DECK BOARDS

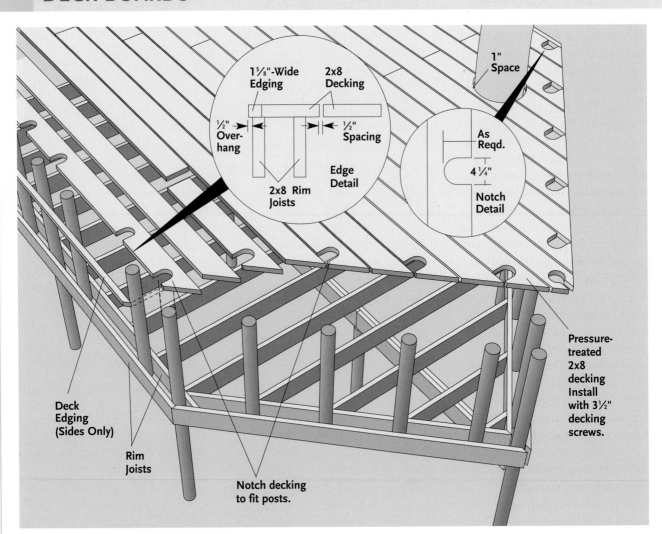

1 5/8"-Wide Edging
2x8 Decking
1/2" Overhang
1/2" Spacing
2x8 Rim Joists
Edge Detail
1" Space
As Reqd.
4 1/4"
Notch Detail
Deck Edging (Sides Only)
Rim Joists
Notch decking to fit posts.
Pressure-treated 2x8 decking Install with 3 1/2" decking screws.

SIDEWALL CONSTRUCTION

Once all the deck boards are installed, lay out the position of the wheelhouse walls on the deck, and snap chalk lines to indicate where they fall. Make sure these lines are square to the end of the deck and to each other.

The drawing, right, shows the position of all the studs and plates on the side walls. The studs and top plates are made of standard construction-grade lumber, while the bottom plate is made of pressure-treated lumber to protect it from water damage. Begin building the walls by cutting all the parts to size. Take special care selecting the stock for the top and bottom plates. Use your straightest material for these components because the straighter the wall plates are, the straighter the finished walls will be.

Tack-nail the two plates together, and mark the stud locations on both at the same time. (This ensures that the studs will be straight once the wall is built.) Separate the top and bottom plates, and space them about 8 feet apart on the deck. Place the studs between the plates and against their layout lines. Then attach them by driving nails through the plates and into the ends of the studs. Cut and install the window header and sill boards as shown. Use 16d galvanized nails to prevent rust from staining the boards.

Once all the components are joined, raise the wall, and nail the bottom plate to the deck using its chalk line as a guide. Attach the end of two braces to the wall, and nail a cleat to the deck alongside the other end of these braces. Hold a level against one of the studs that has a brace attached, and push the wall in or out until it's plumb. Once it is, nail the brace to the deck cleat. Do the same with the other brace.

Then build the other sidewall in the same way. Double-check the distance between the two.

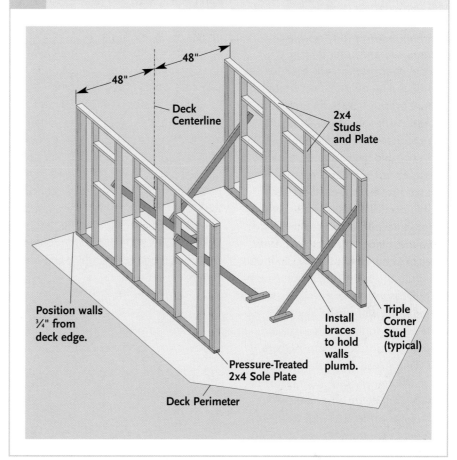

SIDEWALL CONSTRUCTION

48"
48"
Deck Centerline
2x4 Studs and Plate
Position walls ¾" from deck edge.
Install braces to hold walls plumb.
Triple Corner Stud (typical)
Pressure-Treated 2x4 Sole Plate
Deck Perimeter

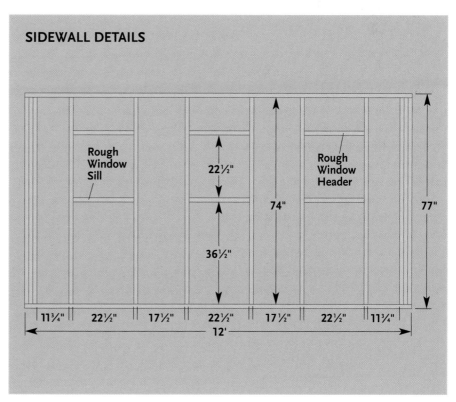

SIDEWALL DETAILS

Rough Window Sill
Rough Window Header
22½"
74"
77"
36½"
11¾" 22½" 17½" 22½" 17½" 22½" 11¾"
12'

BUILDING THE END WALLS

Lay out, cut, and assemble the end walls in the same way you built the side walls. Keep in mind that the best place to build all the walls is on top of the deck. But once the sidewalls are in place and braced, there's not much room to build the end walls. Because of this, consider building the end walls first, and storing them off the deck until the sidewalls are installed. Then just lift the end walls onto the deck, and slide them in place.

Keep in mind that the back end wall is built to the same height as the sidewalls. But the door end wall has two center studs that extend above the top plate height so they can be nailed against the side of the gable rafters. This design feature is necessary because the center of the door is higher than the top of the other walls. The door also comes to a point on the top, so it needs an angled header above it built into the wall. The drawing at right shows how this header is assembled.

Start installing the back end wall by nailing its bottom plate to the deck boards. Then have a helper hold up this wall while you remove the brace (that's closest to the end wall) from one sidewall. This will free up the sidewall so it can be joined to the end wall. Align the corners of the walls so they are square and flush. Then join them together by nailing through the end stud on the end wall into the triple corner stud on the side wall. Do the same thing at the other back-wall corner.

Install the door end wall in the same fashion. Just remember that the bottom plate is attached in two pieces, so it's possible for the two ends of the wall to squeeze together when it's being moved. Before you nail it in place, make sure that the distance between the door opening studs is the same at the bottom and the top.

END WALL CONSTRUCTION

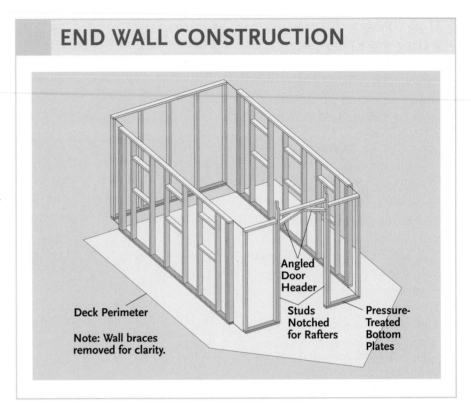

Deck Perimeter

Note: Wall braces removed for clarity.

Angled Door Header

Studs Notched for Rafters

Pressure-Treated Bottom Plates

END WALL DETAILS

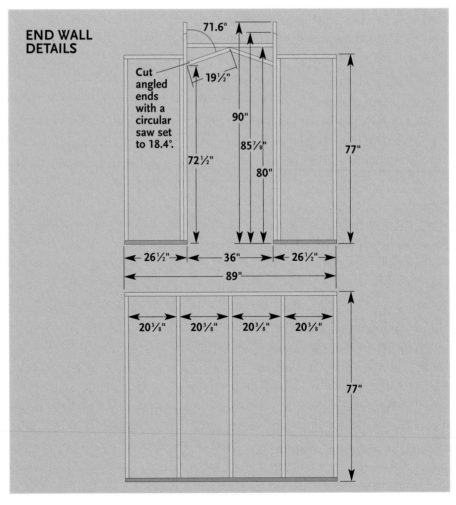

71.6°

Cut angled ends with a circular saw set to 18.4°.

19½"

90"

85⅞"

72½"

80"

77"

26½"   36"   26½"

89"

20⅜"   20⅜"   20⅜"   20⅜"

77"

Once all the corners are joined, check each for plumb, and install diagonal braces on the inside surface of all the walls. These braces will keep the walls plumb until the siding is installed. You should also install a diagonal brace in the center of each sidewall that goes from the top of a stud down to a cleat on the deck floor. Sight down the top plate of each sidewall, and when the top plate looks straight, nail the brace to the cleat. These braces will keep the sidewalls straight until the rafters and collar ties are installed.

INSTALLING THE RAFTERS

The rafters are made of 2x6 construction lumber and are cut to form a 4-in-12 roof pitch. Use the drawing below as a guide for laying out a rafter pattern; then cut the pattern using a circular saw. Use this pattern to mark the rest of the rafters. Once all the rafters are cut, cut a 2x6 to length for the ridge board; then get some help to install these roof components.

Building a small roof like this can be done from stepladders. But it's much easier (and safer) to work from scaffolding. To build a simple platform, just space a pair of sawhorses about 4 feet apart in the middle of the floor. Then nail a 2x4 cleat to the inside of both end walls at the same height as the top of the sawhorses. Nail some planks to the top of the cleats and the sawhorses to create a stable surface from one end of the building to the other.

Begin nailing the rafters in place at both gable ends. Have the helper on top of the scaffolding hold the two rafters up in the air at the approximate height of the ridge board. Then toenail the ends of the rafters to the top plates. Once this first pair is nailed in place, tack-nail the top of the rafters together, and install the rafters at the other gable end. With one person at each gable, re-

move the nails that hold the rafter tops together, and slide the ridge board between the rafters from below.

Align the top edge of the ridge with the top point of each rafter, and check the ridge for level. If it's okay, nail the rafters to the ridge. Install the rest of the rafters in a similar way. The person on the scaffolding should hold the rafter slightly away from the ridge while the person at the wall plate nails the end of the rafter. Then, lower the top of the rafter against the ridge, align the edges

so they are flush, and nail through the ridge board into the end of the rafter.

Finish up the roof framing by installing the collar ties and the gable studs as shown in the drawing below. Then add the plywood roof sheathing to the top of the rafters. These panels are cut to overhang the outside end of the rafters by 1¼ inches. This space allows for a ¾-inch-thick eave trim board and a ½-inch overhang to help carry rainwater away from the top edge of the trim board.

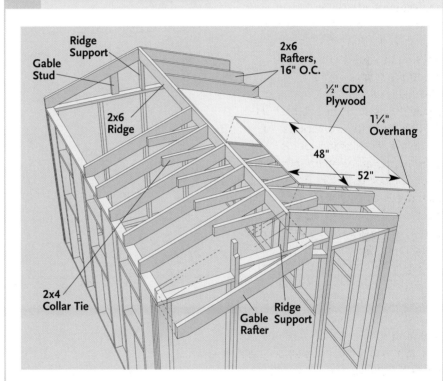

ROOF FRAMING

Ridge Support

Gable Stud

2x6 Ridge

2x4 Collar Tie

2x6 Rafters, 16" O.C.

½" CDX Plywood

1¼" Overhang

48"

52"

Gable Rafter

Ridge Support

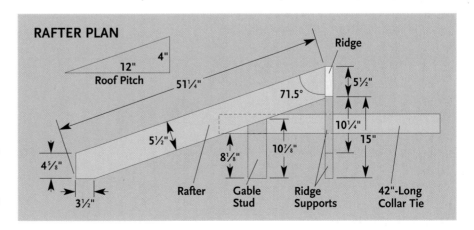

RAFTER PLAN

4"

12"
Roof Pitch

51¼"

Ridge

5½"

71.5°

10¼"

15"

5½"

8⅛"

10⅞"

4⅝"

3½"

Rafter

Gable Stud

Ridge Supports

42"-Long Collar Tie

SIDING, TRIM, AND ROOFING

Once the roof plywood is in place, install the car siding on the wheelhouse walls. This siding is manufactured with ship lap joints, so it's easy to install. Start at the bottom of each wall and leave a ½ inch space between the deck boards and the bottom of the first siding board. This gives rainwater a chance to drain off instead of being trapped against the lumber and causing rot over time. Use 2-½ inch galvanized siding nails (two per board at each stud) for this job.

With careful use of the waste boards as you work, you can minimize the joints in the siding. But where you do need a joint, make sure it falls over the middle of a stud. Stop the siding boards flush with the outside corners of the building. Don't overlap them. Instead, install a piece of ¾-inch quarter-round molding on each corner to add some decoration and to cover up the ends of the siding boards. Also, cut and install the 1x6 trim around the door opening.

After the siding is finished, cut the gable and eave trim boards to size, using 1x8 pine stock. The pattern grids, bottom, show the decorative shapes that must be cut on the bottom edge of each board. To use these grids, just enlarge the squares on the surface of your trim stock, and draw the contoured lines freehand using the squares as a guide. Cut away the waste using a jigsaw and smooth the cut with a spokeshave followed by some 120-grit sandpaper. Nail the trim in place with 16d galvanized casing nails.

Begin the roofing by installing the drip edge along both eaves. Then cover the roof with 30-lb. roofing felt, overlapping the rows by at least 4 inches. After the felt, install pieces of drip edge on both gable ends, then start nailing the shingles in place. We used 3-tab fiberglass asphalt shingles for this job. They

SIDING AND ROOFING

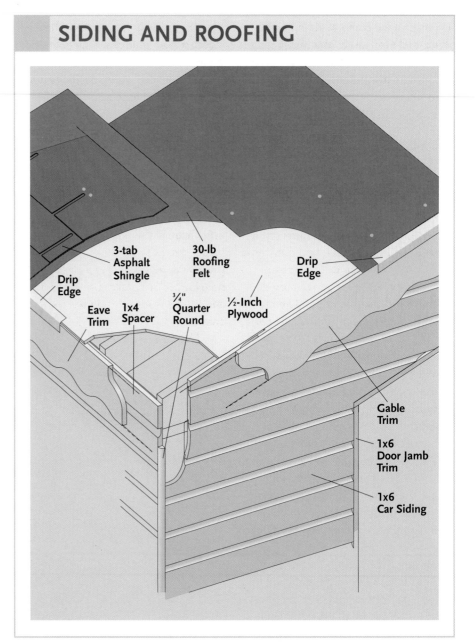

Drip Edge

3-tab Asphalt Shingle

30-lb Roofing Felt

Drip Edge

Eave Trim

1x4 Spacer

¾" Quarter Round

½-Inch Plywood

Gable Trim

1x6 Door Jamb Trim

1x6 Car Siding

TRIM PROFILES

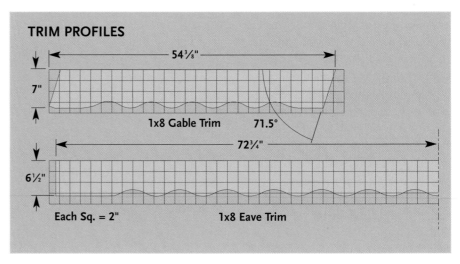

54⅜"

7"

1x8 Gable Trim

71.5°

72¾"

6½"

Each Sq. = 2"

1x8 Eave Trim

are available at home centers, lumber-yards, and even some hardware stores. And, they are inexpensive, long-lasting, and easy-to-install.

BUILDING THE RAILING

The railings around this deck are supported by seven posts that are anchored in the ground, nineteen shorter posts that are sandwiched between the perimeter rim joists, and two short posts that are nailed to the sides of the building. All these posts provide more than enough support. The reason there are so many is that they help create the overall nautical theme of this project's design. These posts suggest pier pilings at the shore.

Another nautical element that is incorporated into the railing is the front prow. This is made of a 2x8 joist that is cut to the size and shape shown in the pattern grid below left. Cut out its curved shape using a jigsaw, and remove the saw marks with a spokeshave and sandpaper. Then cut the 2¼-inch-diameter rope hole using a hole saw.

Once the prow is finished, attach it to the outside of the support post at the end of the deck, using ½ x 6 inch galvanized lag screws and washers. Install three on the outside and one on the inside, making sure to drill a pilot hole for each to make it easier to drive and keep it from splitting the prow board.

The outside of the railing is made of the same car siding boards that are used on the wheelhouse. This project

calls for five courses of siding nailed to the railing posts. Install the first piece so it's ⅛ inch above the surface of the deck to allow rainwater to run underneath. Each section of siding is trimmed with 1½-inch-diameter, lodge-pole pine stock. This material is available at many fencing and landscape suppliers. But if it isn't available in your area, replace it with 2x2 pressure-treated lumber. Attach these trim boards to the posts and the ends of the siding boards with 3-inch galvanized screws as shown in the drawing below.

After all the railing siding and trim have been installed, unroll the 1½-inch-diameter hemp rope, and nail it to the top of each post using 16d galvanized nails. Allow the rope to drape slightly between the posts, trying to keep the dip the same in all the sections.

PROW DETAIL

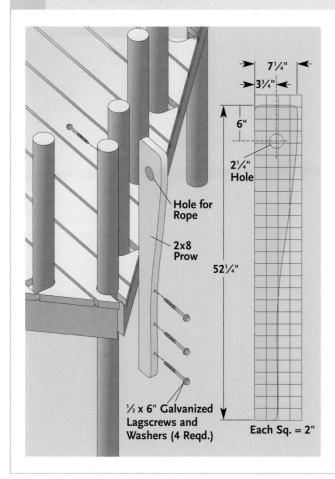

7¼"

3¾"

6"

2¼" Hole

Hole for Rope

2x8 Prow

52¼"

½ x 6" Galvanized Lagscrews and Washers (4 Reqd.)

Each Sq. = 2"

DECK RAILING

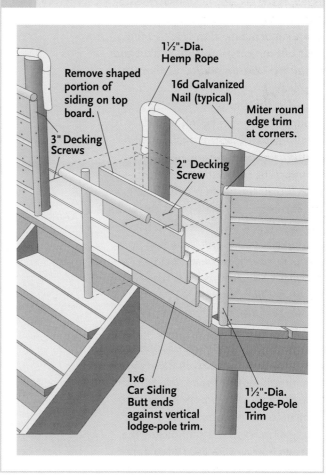

1½"-Dia. Hemp Rope

Remove shaped portion of siding on top board.

16d Galvanized Nail (typical)

Miter round edge trim at corners.

3" Decking Screws

2" Decking Screw

1x6 Car Siding Butt ends against vertical lodge-pole trim.

1½"-Dia. Lodge-Pole Trim

BUILDING THE WHEELHOUSE WINDOWS

The six windows that are located in the side walls of this wheelhouse were custom made for this project. If you're willing to invest in manufactured windows, then simply buy round windows that will fit between the wall studs, and install them before the siding goes on. But if you'd like to save some money, you can build these yourself.

The inner and outer trim rings are made of 2x12 construction lumber. Make sure that the stock you use is very dry; wet stock will split when it dries out. Lay out the circular shapes using the drawing below as a guide, and make the cuts using a jigsaw. Smooth the cuts with rasps and sandpaper. Once the outer ring is sanded smooth, cut a ½-inch radius on the outside edge using a router with a rounding-over bit.

Place the inner ring against the siding so it is centered in the rough opening for the window. Scribe around the ring, and cut out the siding using a jigsaw. Join the inner ring to the back of the outer ring with construction adhesive and 2½-inch galvanized deck screws. Slide this assembly into the hole in the siding, and attach it with deck screws as shown. Apply a thick bead of silicone caulk where the back of the outer ring meets the siding.

Cut a piece of sheet acrylic to size, and place it against the back of the inner ring. Cut the window backer boards to the size and shape that are shown in the drawing, and push these against the acrylic sheet. Hold these backer boards in place with the small retaining strips as shown. Install these with screws driven through the strips and into the window studs, header, and sill. Seal the joint between the inner ring and the acrylic with a bead of clear silicone caulk.

BUILDING THE WHEELHOUSE DOOR

The drawing, opposite, shows the back-side of the door seen from inside the wheelhouse. The door is built to conform to the existing opening, so make careful measurements before you start cutting any lumber. Keep in mind that the door should be assembled so there's a uniform ¼-inch space around it to prevent sticking.

Start the construction by cutting the door boards to size and shape. Then place the vertical boards on a work surface, and arrange the batten boards on the back as shown in the drawing. Attach the battens with 1¼-inch galvanized deck screws, making sure that they are square to the vertical boards.

Also make sure that the sides of the door are square to the bottom of the door. Carefully turn over the door assembly, and drive screws through the front of the vertical boards into the battens.

Next, lay out the position of the window in the door. Mark the 14-inch-diameter porthole on the outside, and cut out the waste using a jigsaw. Sand the cut edges smooth; then turn over the door again; cut the sheet acrylic to size; and place it against the porthole opening as shown. Hold this sheet in place with ½-inch square retaining strips. With the outside of the door facing up, seal the joint between the acrylic and the door boards with silicone caulk, and cut the ornamental mullion strips to size. Apply a thin bead of silicone to the back of these strips, and press against the acrylic window.

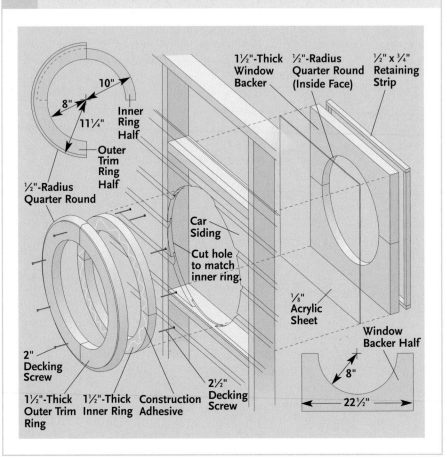

WINDOW DETAIL

10"
8"
11¼"

Inner Ring Half

Outer Trim Ring Half

½"-Radius Quarter Round

1½"-Thick Window Backer

½"-Radius Quarter Round (Inside Face)

½" x ¾" Retaining Strip

Car Siding

Cut hole to match inner ring.

⅛" Acrylic Sheet

Window Backer Half

8"

22½"

2" Decking Screw

1½"-Thick Outer Trim Ring

1½"-Thick Inner Ring

Construction Adhesive

2½" Decking Screw

Attach two 7-inch galvanized strap hinges to the door battens. Then prop the door in the opening, and mark the screw holes for the hinge leaves on the stud and jamb board. Drill screw clearance holes; then hold the door in the opening again, and attach both hinges with their screws. Test the door for proper fit. If it works well and doesn't bind anywhere, then install door stops on the inside surface of the door jambs. Finish up by installing a simple latch as shown in the drawing below.

When the construction is complete, coat the posts, flooring, and siding with a wood-colored stain. Add a color accent by using green stain on the door and the wheelhouse trim.

DOOR DETAIL

¾"-Square Door Stop, 1½" from Inside Jamb Edge

¾"-Square Mullion Strips (Glue to window.)

14"-Dia. Hole

⅛" x 16" x 16" Acrylic Plastic

½"-Square Retaining Strips

4¼" Wide Jamb

16"

16"

5½"

77¼"

Latch

31"

45¾"-Long Brace

Galvanized Strap Hinge

1 x 6 Pine

5½"

4½"

34¼"

resource guide

This list of manufacturers and associations is meant to be a general guide to additional industry and product-related sources. It is not intended as a listing of products and manufacturers represented by the photographs in this book.

American Playscapes
678-367-0491
www.americanplayscapes.com
Sells play systems, swing sets, and accessories.

Backyard Adventures
14201 I-27
Amarillo, TX 79119
806-622-1220
www.backyardadventures.com
Sells play systems and accessories.

BuySwings.com
P.O. Box 22566
Knoxville, TN 37933
888-429-0753
www.buyswings.com
Sells swing sets and accessories.

KNXX Safe Sand Co.
2912 Diamond St.
San Francisco, CA 94131
415-971-1776
www.safesand.com
Sells silica-free sand.

Outdoor Fun Store
877-386-1700
www.outdoorfunstore.com
Sells, installs, and services play systems, swing sets, and accessories.

Planit Play
190 Etowah Industrial Ct.
Canton, GA 30114
866-346-7529
www.planitplay.com
Sells play systems, swing sets, and accessories.

PlayKids
4281 S.W. 75 Ave.
Miami, FL 33155
800-958-5437
www.playkids.com
Sells play systems and accessories.

R & W Rope Warehouse
39 Tarkin Pl.
New Bedford, MA 02745
www.rwrope.com
Sells different varieties of rope for all purposes.

Rainbow Play Systems
800-724-6269
www.rainbowplay.com
Sells play systems and accessories.

Spring Swings & More
2000 Avenue P, Suite 13
Riviera Beach, FL 33404
561-845-6966
www.springswings.com
Sells specialty outdoor, backyard, and residential play products, such as zip lines and spinning swings.

Swing-N-Slide
1212 Barberry Dr.
Janesville, WI 53545
800-888-1232
www.swing-n-slide.com
Sells play systems, swing sets, and accessories.

SwingWorks, Inc.
190 Etowah Industrial Ct.
Canton, GA 30114
877-447-9464
www.swingworks.com
Sells swing sets and accessories.

U.S. Consumer Product Safety Commission
4330 East West Hwy.
Bethesda, MD 20814
800-638-2772
www.cpsc.gov
A government organization that reports information on the safety of and risks associated with products sold in the United States. Download a free "Handbook for Public Playground Safety" from the Web site.

Actual dimensions The exact cross sectional measurements of a piece of lumber after it has been cut, surfaced, and dried. For example, a 2x4s actual dimensions are $1\frac{1}{2}$ x $3\frac{1}{2}$ inches.

Air-dried lumber Wood seasoned by exposure to the air without use of artificial heat.

Architectural scale A three-sided ruler, triangular in cross section, with feet-to-inch conversion scales that allow you to instantly convert measurements in feet to fractions of an inch in creating "scaled" drawings on paper.

Baluster Vertical board or dowel installed between top and bottom rails for safety and decoration.

Bevel An angle cut along the edge or end of a board.

Bevel siding A tapered siding board used as roofing for the Playhouse.

Box nail A slender-shafted nail used when a thicker common nail would otherwise split wood, especially at board ends.

Building code Municipal rules that regulate building practices and procedures. Local building permits are almost always required for new construction or major renovations. Inspections may be required to confirm adherence to codes.

Carriage bolt A round-headed bolt used to fasten wood members face to face. In this book, the threaded part and its nut and washer are recessed in wood whenever the protruding end could otherwise cause injury.

Cleat A small wood piece that supports another wood member.

Concrete At first a semifluid mixture of portland cement, sand (fine aggregate), gravel, or crushed stone that hardens rock solid.

Curing The slow chemical action that hardens concrete. Also describes the air-drying of wood.

Decking Boards nailed to joists to form a deck surface.

Frost line The maximum depth to which soil freezes in winter. Your local building department can provide information of the frost-line depth in your area below which structural supports must be dug to prevent heaving from ice.

Galvanizing Coating a metal with a thin protective layer (e.g., zinc) to prevent rust. Connectors and fasteners should be hot-dipped for outdoor use.

Impact-reducing materials Wood mulch, wood chips, sand, or pea gravel used to soften the landing of a child falling or jumping from any part of a play structure. See page 40.

Joist One of the parallel framing members that support a floor or ceiling.

Kickback The forceful backward reaction of a saw whose blade has met with unplanned resistance, such as from a pinching saw kerf.

Lag screw A large hex-head screw used to fasten framing members face to face; typically used to join horizontal framing members to a post.

Lumber grade A label that reflects the lumber's natural growth characteristics (such as knots), defects that result from milling errors, and manufacturing techniques.

Miter joint A joint in which the ends of two boards are cut at equal angles (typically 45 degrees) to form a corner.

Nominal dimensions The identifying dimensions in inches of a piece of lumber (e.g., 2x4), which are larger than the actual dimensions ($1\frac{1}{2}$ x $3\frac{1}{2}$ inches) after milling.

Penny Unit of measurement (abbr. d) for nail length, such as a 10d nail, which is 3 inches long.

Permit A license issued by local building authorities granting permission to do work on your property.

Pier footing A concrete base encasing or attached to a post.

Plumb Vertically straight.

Plywood A wood panel composed of thin wood layers glued together.

Post Vertical framing member (e.g., a 4x4 or 4x6) set in the ground to support a structure.

Posthole digger A hand tool composed of two hinged, shovel-like parts that loosen soil and then grasp it for removal from postholes.

Power auger A gas-powered tool used for drilling into the ground. Often rented by homeowners to dig multiple postholes.

Premixed concrete Bagged, dry cement, sand, and aggregate that is mixed with water for small jobs, such as securing the base of a post.

Pressure-treated lumber Wood that has had preservatives forced into it under pressure to repel rot and insects.

Rail Horizontal member fastened between posts and used for support or as a barrier.

Ready-mix concrete Wet concrete that arrives by truck ready to pour.

Recess A shallow depression drilled in wood to allow the head or threaded end of a through-bolt to be flush with the wood surface.

Rim joist A joist that runs along the outside of the floor platform.

Rip cut A cut made with the grain on a piece of wood.

Shank The part of a screw or nail that is driven into wood.

Site plan A drawing that maps out your house and yard.

Slat A narrow strip of wood.

Wood preservative Liquid chemical applied to wood to prevent decay and insect attacks.

index

photo credits

All photos Creative Homeowner unless otherwise noted.

page 7: iStockphoto.com/Mary Marin **page 144:** Chris Tubbs/Redcover.com **page 147:** Tony Giammarino/Giammarino & Dworkin **page 161:** iStockphoto.com/Mary Marin **page 173:** Chris Tubbs/Redcover.com

METRIC EQUIVALENTS

Length

1 inch	25.4mm
1 foot	0.3048m
1 yard	0.9144m
1 mile	1.61km

Area

1 square inch	645mm^2
1 square foot	0.0929m^2
1 square yard	0.8361m^2
1 acre	4046.86m^2
1 square mile	2.59km^2

Volume

1 cubic inch	16.3870cm^3
1 cubic foot	0.03m^3
1 cubic yard	0.77m^3

Common Lumber Equivalents

Sizes: Metric cross sections are so close to their U.S. sizes, as noted below, that for most purposes they may be considered equivalents.

Dimensional lumber	1x2	19 x 38mm
	1x4	19 x 89mm
	2x2	38 x 38mm
	2x4	38 x 89mm
	2x6	38 x 140mm
	2x8	38 x 184mm
	2x10	38 x 235mm
	2x12	38 x 286mm
Sheet sizes	4 x 8 ft.	1200 x 2400mm
	4 x 10 ft.	1200 x 3000mm
Sheet thicknesses	¼ in.	6mm
	⅜ in.	9mm
	½ in.	12mm
	¾ in.	19 mm
Stud/joist spacing	16 in. o.c.	400mm o.c.
	24 in. o.c.	600mm o.c.

Capacity

1 fluid ounce	29.57mL
1 pint	473.18mL
1 quart	0.95L
1 gallon	3.79L

Weight

1 ounce	28.35g
1 pound	0.45kg

Temperature

Fahrenheit = Celsius x 1.8 + 32
Celsius = Fahrenheit - 32 x 5⁄9

Nail Size & Length

Penny Size	Nail Length
2d	1"
3d	1¼"
4d	1½"
5d	1¾"
6d	2"
7d	2¼"
8d	2½"
9d	2¾"
10d	3"
12d	3¼"
16d	3½"

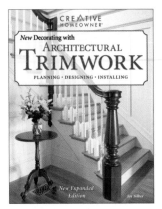
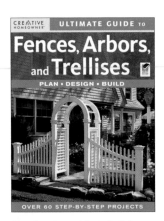
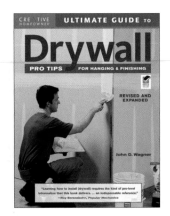
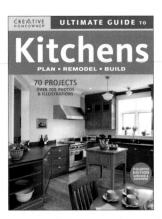
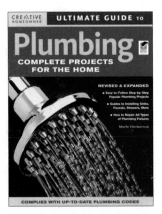
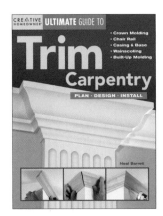

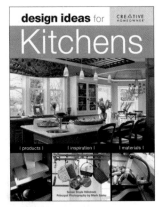
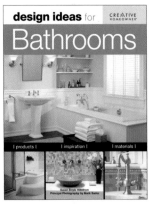